The Fall of Home

*How Mass Migration Is Destroying the West —
and What We Can Do About It*

WALDEN E. LEIF

My children,

you shall inherit the Earth —

may it still be worthy of your love.

Contents

1

I Remember

I remember what it was like 30 years ago, growing up in a small village in England.

The streets, the schools, the sense of belonging. Village greens where kids played until dusk. Wandering down to the local pub for a quiet pint and a bit of small talk with the regulars, or just a paper and a moment to yourself. Brisk walks along winding country lanes after Sunday lunch, neatly trimmed hedgerows blurring past in the autumn air. Marching into town with the weekend crowd to cheer on the football team. Clutching a thermos of soup while the bonfire crackled into the November sky. The harvest festival in the local town square. A Christingle service in the same church where you were baptised.

The English countryside, there's nothing like it. That land shaped me. Walking beneath low grey skies, mist cutting through the woods, the air thick with damp earth. It's not just scenery, it's home. Emerald green fields, ancient oaks, moss-covered brick walls — they speak a language I understand without effort.

I don't wear rose-tinted glasses. It wasn't paradise. But it was rooted. It meant something. It held a shape you could recognise. A rhythm you could grow up inside.

I was there before Tony Blair, the newly elected Labour Prime Minister, threw open the doors in the late '90s. Before this social experiment began. Before everything started to change.

You don't notice a civilisation vanish in a single moment. You notice it in fragments. When you walk through your old neighbourhood and feel like a tourist. When the streets no longer sound like home. When cherished traditions vanish quietly, and you're told that noticing it makes you a bad person.

That's how our culture dies. Not with conquest. With consent. With polite silence. There's no great event. No revolution. No declaration that something has ended. The collapse doesn't come with a bang. It comes with a shrug. Not through war, but indifference.

You're not imagining things. You're not hateful for noticing. You're not wrong to want your country to feel like your country. Your grandparents built something. They worked. Fought. Sacrificed. They gave you a gift. And somewhere along the way, it became fashionable to call it progress to give it away. Yet this isn't destiny. Deep down, we all feel what's been lost.

Mass migration isn't just a cultural issue. It's a historic failure of governance across the Western world, with cascading consequences. A failure to secure borders. A failure of political will. A failure to plan, prioritise, or protect the public interest. Whether through neglect or design, it's mismanagement on a civilisational scale.

One thing that often goes unspoken about mass migration and the ideology that enables it is the distinct cruelty it entails. Not the obvious kind, but something colder, more detached. Of course, being open-minded toward immigrants or respectful of other cultures (within reason) is admirable. I support that. Being well-travelled, learning from others, embracing what's worth embracing — that's a good instinct.

However, the ideology of top-down cultural displacement, imposed without consent, in defiance of public will, and despite clear warnings of social fracture, is something altogether different. It's brutal in its indifference. To steamroll democratic resistance, to pretend that national identity is irrelevant, to treat people's homes as if they belong to someone else — there's something quietly inhuman about it. A cold, bureaucratic kind of violence.

But let's get a few things straight: this book is not a treatise on "the great replacement theory." It's not a white nationalist manifesto. It's not a call to seal the borders. And it's not a denial that immigration, done right, can be a good thing.

I like immigration, in controlled moderation. I consider myself fairly cosmopolitan. I've lived in multiple countries. I like learning about other cultures, trying new food, and hearing different stories. But I also like my own culture. I think it's worth preserving. And somehow, saying this makes me "far right." Why?

I don't think Western nations should be expected to absorb the world's every crisis. I don't want hijabs normalised in primary schools. I don't want Shakespeare to be "decolonised." And I'd quite like my kids to afford a home, without being taxed to house the population of Afghanistan.

This book exists because you're not imagining things. You're not backward, and you're certainly not alone. What you are is gaslit. As Douglas Murray described, there's a pattern to how dissent is crushed:

"First, that it isn't happening, that what you are seeing with your eyes you are not seeing; second, that it is happening but it is good for you; third, that it may not be good for you but you deserve it; and finally — it doesn't matter, because it's going to happen anyway."

That's the quiet directive beneath it all: stay silent, stop resisting, and accept the transformation of your country. This book is for those who sense something is deeply wrong, yet are told not to question it. For the politically displaced. For the liberals mugged by reality. For anyone who still believes a nation should feel like home.

Mass migration is a catastrophe for the West. You never voted for it, and when people have been given the chance, they've overwhelmingly rejected it.

When someone says, *"multiculturalism doesn't work,"* they're not citing theory. They're naming a lived reality. A quiet, mounting recognition that something fundamental has broken. That the story they were sold no longer matches the world around them. What they usually mean is simple:

There's too much immigration. It's the wrong kind of immigration. And the newcomers aren't integrating.

Strip away the slogans and sentimentality, and the issue boils down to three key factors: volume, quality, and assimilation.

In the UK, a 2025 YouGov poll found that 70% of the public believe immigration levels are too high, with half naming it a top-tier political issue [1]. In France, a 2023 survey by IFOP, one of the country's leading polling agencies, reported that 70% of citizens believe there are "too many foreigners" in France, despite decades of official pro-diversity messaging [2].

In Germany, a 2024 poll by Infratest dimap for the public broadcaster ARD found that 52% of respondents support mass deportations of failed asylum seekers and illegal migrants [3].

In the United States, Gallup surveys conducted regularly since the early 2000s have shown a consistent majority in favour of stricter border enforcement [4]. In Canada, a 2024 Environics survey found that 58% of respondents believe the country accepts too many immigrants, the highest level of concern in more than 25 years [5]. Additionally, only 33% of Canadians said immigration enriches national culture [6].

However, it continues to happen anyway, imposed from above with no regard for the public's will. Worse, if you dare question it, you're smeared as a racist. The message is clear: you don't get a choice, and you're not allowed to complain.

Mass migration is the defining issue of the 21st century. It's not just one issue among many; it's the root of countless downstream problems: cultural fragmentation, rising crime, financial strain, and political destabilisation.

Western Europe has been patient zero. The poster child of a borderless, globalist experiment. And what's been the result? Overwhelmed schools. Stressed hospitals. Fractured communities. Massive increase in sexual assaults and violent crime. And yet, we're told this is progress.

This is why the Reform Party is gaining popularity in the UK. Why Marine Le Pen or the AfD are no longer fringe. Why Trump's most popular policy isn't tax cuts — it's deportations. Because deep down, people know: if you don't control who comes in, you lose everything. Your streets, your culture, your country. It's that simple.

Mass migration isn't normal, and it's not inevitable. It's a political choice, made by people who rarely pay the cost. This book is for when your liberal friend, who treats *The Guardian* like gospel, starts parroting the usual lines:

"We're a nation of immigrants!"
"Diversity is our strength!"
"They're just coming for a better life!"
"You just don't like brown people."

You've heard all the excuses. That's why I wrote this book — to help you push back. With clarity. With confidence. Without apology. Because the truth is, you are the one paying the price. In cities that grow more chaotic by the day. In rising crime. In strained public services. In the steady collapse of trust between neighbours.

Mass migration erodes the very foundations that make nations thrive. It transforms high-trust societies into low-trust ones, where suspicion replaces solidarity. It fractures coherent cultures into fragmented, balkanised enclaves with competing values and little shared identity. It drains wealth, turning once prosperous countries into overburdened welfare states. And it takes safe, familiar streets and fills them with unease, crime, and a growing sense that home no longer feels like home.

And when you speak up? You become the problem. You're told to repent — for history, for privilege, for colonialism. Told your culture isn't worth preserving, that you don't even have one. That your future must be offered up to prove your virtue.

This book says no. You don't owe anyone your country. You don't have to "do better." You don't have to pretend this is working. Because it isn't. The West is being hollowed out from within, by a policy no one chose, enforced by people who live far from its consequences—the ultimate luxury belief.

Of course, mass migration does work for some people. It enriches the top: cheap labour for corporations, loyal votes for "progressives," and a fragmented society that's easier to manage. Our ruling class has no loyalty to nation, place, or tradition — only to capital and self-interest.

It also works for people coming over; benefits, housing, or they wouldn't come. It just doesn't work for you. You get the bill: higher taxes, lower wages, broken communities.

How badly it doesn't work for you depends on your wealth and class. If you're middle-class in the UK, you live in a leafy village in Surrey, drive a Land Rover to a Pakistani curry house once a month to give little private school–educated Alfie and Lulu a taste of something exotic, then head back to safety. How lovely. If you're working-class, you live on a grotty estate that's become increasingly hostile. Social services are overwhelmed. Wages are suppressed. Schools push foreign ideology. Your local councillors despise you. And to top it off, your underage daughters are targeted in industrial-scale grooming scandals.

Speak the truth online, and you risk censorship, bans, and even prison. This is why the middle class doesn't just miss the point — they help enforce the lie. They're often the loudest voices in favour of mass migration. But notice: they're not moving to Luton, where their ideals take form. They remain in their leafy postcodes, sipping lattes and signalling virtue from a safe distance.

They live in luxury belief bubbles, insulated from the costs of the ideology they champion (for now). It's easy to cheer from a detached house in zone 3. Easy to preach inclusion when your kids aren't in classrooms crippled by chaos. Easy to talk about diversity when you don't live in a postcode defined by it. For the working class, it's not a belief. It's a burden.

None of this comes from hatred. It comes from a basic human instinct — to protect what you love. The people who built this country deserve loyalty. So do their children. This isn't about race. It's about limits. About culture, cohesion, and consent. About the fundamental right of a people to say: enough.

Danes are slated to be a minority in Denmark by 2096. It should be completely uncontroversial to believe that the majority of the population in Denmark should be Danish. The same goes for Ireland, Scotland, Finland, Poland, and Hungary.

This topic isn't abstract for me. I know what it was like before. I remember taking the train down from the countryside to visit London regularly in my youth — once the greatest city in the world, now an absolute shadow of its former self. London, the city of smoky jukebox pubs and red postboxes. Of pigeons scattering in Trafalgar Square. Of West End matinees and hot bags of fish and chips eaten on a bench as the city buzzed around you. Buckingham Palace, Westminster Abbey, Shakespeare's Globe. It wasn't clean or perfect, but it had character, layers of it, baked into the bricks and echoing through the alleys. You'd get the Overground to Gospel Oak, stroll down to Parliament Hill, and look out over a skyline that felt both ancient and alive. The city spoke every dialect of British life — working-class banter, upper-crust drawl — and it all fit. London wasn't just a city; it was a story you could step into.

What's happened since isn't progress. It's a slow, deliberate erasure of the city (and country) I knew. One of the most radicalising things you can do is simply see what life was like not too long ago. You don't need to go back to the 1950s. Just watch a film set in London in the early 2000s. The difference is staggering. The streets, the faces, the culture — it's all recognisably British. Fast-forward two decades, and you'll struggle to find the same city. It's hard to overstate the scale and speed of the transformation.

It's a civilisational trauma, watching 1,000 years of identity, history, and sacrifice dismantled in a single generation by politicians too ashamed to defend what they inherited, and too cowardly to admit what they've destroyed.

This book isn't just about Britain. It's about the West — Europe and the broader Anglosphere — because every Western nation has been subjected to the same social experiment. The same demographic upheaval. The same moral blackmail. Whether it's England, Sweden, France, Germany, Canada, or the United States, the pattern is unmistakable.

This book is for those who are tired of being silenced, smeared, or gaslit. It's for those ready to speak plainly, hold their ground, and stop apologising. Every nation has the right to decide who enters. Only the West is shamed for exercising that right.

These are the arguments to reclaim it — because there is no endpoint. No moment when they say, *"That's enough diversity."* They'll keep screaming *"too white"* until your street looks like a joint venture between Karachi and Mozambique, and even then, the media will call it a vibrant success story.

To date, Western nations have been remarkably restrained. But that patience is reaching a breaking point. The quiet stoicism of the West is often mistaken for agreement. But that's a dangerous assumption. In town after town, ordinary people are beginning to resist, sometimes in whispers, sometimes in protest. Not because they are hateful. But because no one listened when they spoke softly.

I believe Britain is entering pre-revolutionary territory, but not in the way past revolutions have unfolded. This feels less like a radical upheaval aimed at creating something new and more like a conservative counter-revolution. A revolt not to remake society, but to reclaim it. To overthrow what many now perceive as a temporary, hostile, occupying regime, an elite detached from the people, and to restore something older, rooted, and recognisably British.

From Spain, Ireland, France, Portugal, England, and Greece to Germany, 2025 has seen a surge of riots, violence, and unrest. The public sees what the ruling class won't admit: unchecked mass migration is fuelling chaos, crime, and collapse. If voices aren't heard at the ballot box, they will be on the street.

Years ago, David Betz, a war theorist and professor at King's College London, warned that Western states were drifting toward civil war. He called it "visual war," a conflict waged through images that erodes trust, legitimacy, and national cohesion. When identity fractures and belief in the system collapses, violence follows.

"We are not on the brink of civil war," he wrote, *"we are in the early stages of one."*

When people are ignored long enough, when they're told their home no longer belongs to them, they stop asking. They stop waiting. One day, they will erupt, and when they do, the ruling class will feign surprise. But they were warned.

But before we can fully grasp the scale of the crisis, we need to define it clearly. What exactly do we mean by "mass migration"? And how is it different from the immigration most people are willing to accept?

2

What Mass Migration Really Means

I remember walking the South Bank as a young man, wind off the Thames, St. Paul's rising in the distance. London felt alive, layered, familiar, still unmistakably British. It was diverse, but there was a shared grammar. Now I walk those same streets and feel like I've crossed a border. The change isn't just visual. It's atmospheric. You don't need statistics to notice it. You feel it in your bones.

London has always been an international hub, a centre of global trade. It was never a monoculture. But the past 40 years have brought something very different. Not just more immigrants, but a wholesale demographic and cultural transformation, driven by scale, speed, and policy rather than organic exchange.

Concern about mass migration isn't about Stacey from Poland, who moved to the UK in 2006 to become a nurse, paid her taxes, and built a life. It's not about small numbers of high-skilled, culturally compatible individuals who assimilate and contribute. That kind of immigration — controlled, selective, mutually beneficial — is something most people, including those labelled "anti-immigration," can accept.

Mass migration is something else entirely. It refers to the large-scale, often unvetted movement of people from poor, unstable, or culturally incompatible regions into wealthy Western nations. It's typically facilitated by lax border enforcement, broken asylum systems, and governments too cowardly or too ideologically captured to act in the public interest. It is not controlled. It is not strategic. It is not sustainable.

We're talking about illegal border crossings. No vetting. No background checks. No invitation. We're talking about fake asylum seekers — people who claim persecution, only to return to their home countries for vacation once they've secured residency. If your homeland is safe enough for a holiday, it wasn't unsafe enough to justify asylum. Others pass through multiple safe countries just to reach the UK or Germany, where the benefits are most accessible. Free housing. Free legal aid. Free healthcare. No paperwork required.

Then there are the economic migrants who pose as refugees because they know the rules are looser. The students and tourists who overstay their visas and simply vanish into the system. Western governments rarely track them, let alone deport them.

But it's not just visa overstays. There's a more organised pipeline, one that the government openly supports. That pipeline runs through the universities. These institutions actively recruit international students — not for academic excellence, but for profit. They charge overseas applicants steep fees, often double those of domestic students, in exchange for a student visa. Once enrolled, many students complete low-rigor courses and then seamlessly transition to post-study work visas. The result? A long-term path to permanent settlement, all rubber-stamped by the state. Nearly two million immigrants have entered the UK through this channel in the past five years.

One person gets in, and soon ten more follow: parents, siblings, cousins, none of whom were selected for skills, character, or compatibility. This is chain migration. And it doesn't have to be illegal to be harmful.

We've been taught to believe that as long as someone filled out the right form, their presence is automatically legitimate. But that's a lie. Laws can be wrong. Policies can be suicidal. Demographic change doesn't need to come at the point of a sword to be catastrophic. It can arrive wrapped in bureaucracy, waved through by civil servants, and funded by taxpayers.

Too many work permits, too many international students, too many H1Bs — all can be detrimental if not limited and carefully managed. Because even legal migration, scaled recklessly, can hollow out a nation just as surely as illegal entry. It shifts the labour market, rewires the culture, and dilutes the very identity it's joining.

I remember reading about a story from Glasgow, a city once known for its hospitality, now stretched to breaking point. In 2025, the city council warned that the UK's asylum system was placing "unprecedented pressure" on local services and threatening severe damage to social cohesion.

At a public meeting, a mother of three described being turned away from an overcrowded clinic twice in one week — while newly arrived asylum seekers were seen first. A local teacher reported that half of her class had stopped showing up. Recent arrivals. No documents. No housing. No plan. By that point, Glasgow had taken in over 4,000 asylum seekers. The city had run out of flats. Run out of budget. But still the buses came.

"We just don't have enough flats," said one council worker. *"Every week, it's another busload, and we're being told to house them before anyone else. Locals are angry. They feel forgotten."*

Councillors begged for a pause. For support. For some way to cope. None came.

That story stuck with me — not because it was dramatic, but because it wasn't. It was quiet. Bureaucratic. Ordinary. No protests. No headlines. Just institutions quietly buckling while the people who built them waited, unheard. That's the real face of mass migration. Not just the boats. It's the town where the hospital waitlist doubles. The school that can't cope. The citizen who's told, again, to wait their turn in a country they helped build.

Across the West, the numbers speak for themselves.

In 2023, net migration to the UK reached 685,000, just shy of the record 764,000 the year before [7] [8]. That's the equivalent of adding a city the size of Glasgow every single year. And it's happening while Britain faces a crippling housing crisis, overwhelmed schools, and strained public services. Over 85% of these arrivals came from non-EU countries — many with no historical or cultural connection to Britain [8][9]. The majority were not high-skilled workers. Most arrived to study, claim asylum, or reunite with family [9][10]. Immigration is now the sole driver of population growth, pushing Britain's numbers up by over 1% a year [11].

At the same time, Channel crossings continue to surge. Nearly 20,000 migrants arrived in "small boats" between January and June 2025 alone. In 2024, the total reached almost 37,000 — a 25% increase over the previous year [12].

One in four schools in England is now majority non-white. In London, White British people make up just 36.8% of the population, according to the 2021 Census [13]. And if current trends continue, Professor Matt Goodwin projects that White British people will become a minority nationwide by 2063 [14]. To put all this into perspective: in

1960, Britain was approximately 99% white. A shift of that magnitude, without war, famine, or plague, is historically unprecedented.

In Germany, 1.4 million migrants arrived in 2023. That includes 351,915 asylum applications, the highest since the 2015 migrant crisis [15]. The foreign-born population now exceeds 15 million, nearly 19% of the total [15]. Most of the asylum seekers are young males from Syria, Afghanistan, and Turkey, groups with low employment rates and poor integration outcomes.

Ireland, with a population of just over 5 million, now has nearly 1 million residents who were born outside the country, accounting for almost one in five of its population [16]. In Dublin, that number rises to nearly one in three. Migration has accounted for all of Ireland's population growth in recent years. Without it, the population would be declining. Between 2015 and today, 736,377 non-EU migrants have been added to the Irish population. Over the same period, the government has issued 1.3 million Personal Public Service (PPS) numbers to non-Irish nationals. Between 2022 and 2023 alone, net migration reached a record 77,600. Migrants have come from India, Brazil, Nigeria, and other culturally distant countries.

Canada admitted 471,771 permanent residents in 2023, a record high [17]. In the first three quarters of 2024, 483,590 new permanent residents had already been admitted [18]. As of October 1, 2024, Canada hosted over 3 million non-permanent residents, accounting for approximately 7.4% of the total population [18]. Canada experienced its fastest population growth in 66 years in 2023. The population increased by 1.27 million people, with 97.6% of that growth driven by international migration [18]. As of 2025, about one-fifth of the private sector workforce is "temporary" foreign workers.

In Sweden, a nation of just 10 million, the foreign-born population now accounts for 20.6%, and an additional 11% have two foreign-born parents [19]. That means over one in three Swedes has recent immigrant ancestry. Sweden has accepted more than 2 million migrants since the 1990s. Gang violence, shootings, and bombings are now common. Immigrant unemployment remains double the national average.

In the United States, there were over 2.4 million migrant encounters at the southwest border in 2023 alone [20]. During the Biden presidency in 2021, border encounters reached a record high of 8.5 million. An estimated 1.7 million "gotaways" — migrants who entered undetected — are believed to be inside the U.S. The total number of illegal immigrants is estimated between 11 and 20 million. Most are unvetted, rarely deported, and many strain schools, hospitals, and housing.

The American H-1B visa program, originally meant to fill genuine skill gaps, has been radically abused. Over 70 percent of H-1B visas are awarded to Indian nationals, primarily in the tech sector. Major corporations, such as Microsoft and Disney, lay off domestic workers and then apply for thousands of H-1 B visas to replace them with cheaper foreign labour. It's not about merit, it's about margins. The system rewards obedience over talent. H-1B workers are tied to their employers and risk deportation if they leave, making them cheaper, more compliant, and easier to control. Wages are suppressed, and domestic workers are pushed out.

As of the 2020 U.S. Census, White Americans are now a minority in all ten of the country's largest cities — New York, Los Angeles, Chicago, Houston, Phoenix, Philadelphia, San Antonio, San Diego, Dallas, and San Jose [21]. This marks a dramatic shift from the 1960s, when these urban centres were often 80 to 90 percent White. In just a few generations, the demographic foundations of America's major cities have undergone a complete transformation, reshaping not only their cultural character but also the political, economic, and social dynamics that once defined them.

This is all happening in plain sight. Demographic upheaval, social fragmentation, and cultural transformation. None of it was voted on, nor was there a mandate from the native populations. And yet we're told this is "who we are." That this is "normal." That opposing it is racist. We're not allowed to ask why, or who benefits.

Every justification for mass migration is just a convenient excuse — a rotating list of talking points meant to pacify public concern while pushing the same agenda. First, it's "We need more workers," then "We need to save the pension system," then "They're only temporary," then "It's a humanitarian crisis." It's Schrödinger's migrant: simultaneously a traumatised dependent and an economic asset. A victim in need of rescue, and a worker ready to power the economy. It's incoherent. And it's false.

In previous generations, immigration meant proving one's value, demonstrating willingness to assimilate, and being invited in. Today, people arrive illegally and demand to stay. They don't adopt the culture. They expect the host society to bend. Many come from places where women are property, where free speech is punished, where gay people are stoned, and where democracy is a foreign concept. Our governments don't just tolerate this. They subsidise it. It takes a special kind of delusion to believe that importing people who are hostile to our values, and dependent on our welfare systems, is a recipe for peace or prosperity.

We cling to old myths and tell ourselves stories written in sepia tones. Ellis Island. The American Dream. The plucky immigrant working three jobs and learning English at night. But that story isn't what's playing out today. Today, we see asylum fraud, chain migration, and welfare dependency. A swelling underclass with no interest in joining the mainstream. The myth is comforting. But the reality is collapse.

Not all migration is equal. And it never was. It's not about race. It's about compatibility, contribution, and consent. Small numbers of people with shared values can integrate. Britain has seen that. British Sikhs, Poles, and Vietnamese refugees have largely assimilated. They speak the language. They work. They contribute. They don't demand special rights. They don't build parallel societies. They become British.

That's what civilisational affinity looks like. The closer a newcomer is — culturally, religiously, temperamentally — to the host population, the smoother the integration. A Lithuanian or Estonian will find their place far more easily in Britain than a Somali or Pakistani. Not because one group is better, but because one shares the language, the customs, even the rhythms of life. The other doesn't. That's why Poland accepts Ukrainian refugees, not Syrians. It's not racism, it's realism.

Even when the numbers are smaller and the cultural distance narrower, assimilation isn't guaranteed. In the 1950s and 1960s, the UK accepted Caribbean migrants from the Commonwealth, known as the Windrush generation. They spoke English. They admired Britain. They genuinely wanted to integrate. And the numbers were low enough for that to happen. Many of their children identified as British and contributed meaningfully to national life.

And yet even that hasn't been an unqualified success. People of Caribbean descent in the UK are statistically more likely to rely on welfare and be involved in crime compared to the national average [22]. Today, Black Britons in London comprise approximately 13.5% of the city's population [23]. Yet, the Metropolitan Police Commissioner has reported that Black males aged 16 to 24 account for nearly 47% of all knife crime offenders in London [24]. That should stand as a warning. If integration struggles at that scale, with that level of cultural proximity, what happens when we bring in millions of people who don't speak the language, don't share the values, and often don't even like the host nation?

You don't get a melting pot. You get a pressure cooker. Many immigrants, even those in their second or third generation, remain loyal to their ancestral identity over the nation in which they live. They reject integration, but refuse to leave.

Pakistani Brits still wave the Pakistani flag. Still cheer for Pakistan over England in cricket. Second and third generations still speak with Pakistani accents. Still marry inside the tribe. Still live in cultural enclaves. More British Muslims have gone off to fight for ISIS than have enlisted in the British Army. These aren't signs of a healthy dual identity. They are symptoms of a civilisational split—a quiet, enduring refusal to belong.

And through all this, the government points to "net migration" and says the numbers are balanced—one out, one in. A British engineer leaves for Singapore. An Eritrean goat herder arrives in Croydon. Job done. A productive, taxpaying British citizen leaving for Dubai is counted the same as a non-English speaking welfare claimant arriving from Somalia. But it's not even close. You can't swap out a Rolls-Royce for a wheelbarrow and call it even. Net migration ignores skills, values, language, and economic contribution. It hides the true impact of who we're losing, and who we're gaining.

But mass migration isn't just a failure of policy or planning. It's the logical outcome of a deeper worldview, one that sees people not as citizens, but as economic inputs. It doesn't matter if it works for the public. It matters if it works on a spreadsheet. Because to them, this isn't chaos. It's a system. And you're just a number in it.

3

The Gospel of Globalism

To understand why mass migration persists despite its obvious downsides, consider how our leaders perceive us. To them, we're not a people. We're not a culture. We're not families with roots, rituals, and a shared sense of belonging. We're economic units. Interchangeable. Movable. Replaceable.

This is the globalist vision: a borderless world, managed by unelected technocrats, where nations are little more than commercial agreements, and populations are treated like a workforce spreadsheet — hire, fire, relocate. A Global tapestry of Interchangeable economic units

The cathedral has been replaced by the consultant. The altar by the algorithm. Low birthrate? No problem, import a million. Aging population? Ship in bodies to pay into the pension pot (even though, as we'll see, they're often a net cost).

In 2015, Canada's WEF member Prime Minister Justin Trudeau declared that Canada is the world's *"first post-national state"* and that it has *"no core identity, no mainstream in Canada"* [25].

Trudeau and his class don't believe in a real Canada. Not as a coherent culture. Not as an extension of a historic people. For them, Canada is a project of moral atonement, a blank slate to be filled by the world's problems and governed by progressive guilt.

That's why they're so comfortable tearing down statues, renaming schools, and rewriting history as an endless tale of colonial sins. They don't see Canada as something to preserve; they see it as something to dismantle. This is the natural endpoint of inherited guilt. Not just multiculturalism, but non-culture. Not just immigration, but replacement as redemption.

The same ideological rot runs through Europe. Elites there, too, have abandoned the idea of the nation as something sacred or worth defending. They claim to uphold democracy, but only when it delivers the outcome they want. When voters lean nationalist or anti-migration, the mask slips and the system moves to crush dissent through lawfare, media smear campaigns, and institutional force.

In France, Marine Le Pen has been dragged through years of politically motivated prosecutions. In Germany, the AfD, now one of the country's most popular parties, is facing calls for an outright ban. In Romania, the anti-migration candidate Calin Georgescu was arrested after a suspect election that tilted in favour of the pro-EU candidate. Shortly after the outcome was secured, the European Union pledged €1 billion to "integrate" hundreds of thousands of migrants, mostly from Arab and African nations, set to arrive under the EU's new Asylum and Migration Pact.

It's hard to look at the damage these policies have caused and the way politicians continue to forge ahead despite widespread public concern, still seeing it all as a series of innocent mistakes. At some point, the pattern becomes too consistent to ignore. National resistance is sidelined. Demographic change is accelerated without consent. Sovereignty is eroded not just through neglect, but through the active subversion of democratic processes. And all of it is cloaked in the language of rights, inclusion, and progress.

It may sound conspiratorial, but after years of the same outcomes, the same evasions, and the same contempt for public will, it's hard not to conclude that this is what our ruling class wants. It's ideological.

In the UK, the strongest evidence for conspiracy came not from critics, but from Labour's own ranks. In October 2009, Andrew Neather – a speechwriter for Tony Blair, Jack Straw, and David Blunkett – published an article in the *Evening Standard* that accidentally gave the game away.

Immigration, he wrote, *"didn't just happen; the deliberate policy of Ministers from late 2000... was to open up the UK to mass immigration."*

Neather was in the room in September 2001, drafting the landmark speech by then–Immigration Minister Barbara Roche. He later recalled *"coming away from some discussions with the clear sense that the policy was intended – even if this wasn't its main purpose – to rub the Right's nose in diversity and render their arguments out of date."*

Even Neather admitted that it seemed "a manoeuvre too far." And the result is now undeniable. Even Blair's favourite think tank, the Institute for Public Policy Research, concedes: *"It is no exaggeration to say that immigration under New Labour has changed the face of the country."*

The same playbook is unfolding across Europe — different actors, same outcome. Look at Serbia; as of July 2025, youth unemployment sits at 20 percent. Yet the government is preparing to bring in 100,000 Ghanaian migrants under a new labour agreement. Why?

Not because the people demanded it, but because foreign NGOs and global agencies have turned Serbia into a test site. The UNHCR, IOM, and EU-linked programs push "humanitarian resettlement" while bypassing public debate entirely. Serbia, eager for EU accession and foreign aid, plays along. It accepts the migrants, takes the money, and sells out its future.

The public hears the same tired script: demographic decline, labour shortages, moral duty. Never mind that local youth can't find work. Never mind that the culture and cohesion of small towns are being transformed without consent. This isn't progress. It's obedience. A small country made compliant through pressure, financial incentives, and ideological manipulation.

Why is the EU so committed to policies that clearly undermine its own member states? Why force mass migration onto nations that never asked for it? Why criminalise opposition and equate dissent with hate? At some point, it becomes impossible to argue this is a bug, not a feature.

EU technocrats do not want strong, self-determining nations. They want compliant provinces within a managed continental system. Strip away identity, weaken resistance, and make every person interchangeable. This is not mismanagement. It is a method. A managed decline, designed to ensure that no European country can ever stand truly independent again.

Where does this ideology come from? Look at Brexit. When Britain voted to leave the EU, it was a thunderclap. Proof that a nation could reject the project and chart its own course. But the political class and civil service saw it as a crisis. Something had to be done to prevent a domino effect.

The response was swift and deliberate. Accelerate migration, destabilise social cohesion, and use the resulting disruption to justify further centralisation. Both Labour and the Conservatives backed this vision. That's why the Channel crossings exploded after Brexit.

A global technocratic system cannot tolerate sovereign nations. European nation-states must be weakened, economically, demographically, and culturally, before any "progress" can be made.

After World War II, the Western world made a fateful decision. In the ruins of fascism and genocide, it wasn't just totalitarianism that was rejected; it was identity itself. Nationalism, tribal loyalty, and strong cultural attachment were seen as dangerous forces. Too much belief, too much belonging, too much memory — this was the new threat.

To prevent future conflict, the post-war order aimed to dismantle these forces entirely. What philosopher R.R. Reno calls the *"strong gods"* — those binding ideals of nation, religion, ancestry, heritage, and meaning — were subdued in the name of peace. In their place came a new gospel: openness, fluidity, deracination, rootlessness.

The dream was simple: peace through placelessness, harmony through homogenisation, stability under an ever-expanding, globally managed technocratic order.

This is the operating system we've been running ever since. The Open Society: globalism as virtue and national identity as original sin. Western pride replaced by permanent apology. Popularised by the ideas of Karl Popper, then given institutional force through the influence of figures like George Soros and organisations like the WEF. Borders became barriers. Sovereignty became selfishness. And any pushback was labelled dangerous.

But that moral software, designed to prevent another Hitler, has left the West defenceless in the face of a very different threat: civilisational surrender. Because not everyone disarmed. The strong gods never left. They just moved — to mosques, to migrant enclaves, to foreign ideologies that are anything but rootless.

And now, with those old loyalties stripped away, the people who built the West are treated like parts in a supply chain — interchangeable, disposable, replaceable. But people are not widgets. You can't swap out a bricklayer from Birmingham with one from rural Bangladesh and expect the same social fabric and cultural continuity.

The idea that you can replace a nation's dominant ethnic group and still maintain its culture is as naive as anything dreamed up by communists. Culture doesn't float in the air. It flows from people. Change the people, and you change the culture. A nation is not magic soil. It's soul. And you don't preserve a soul by replacing the people who carry it. It is not defined by lines on a map or the GDP it generates. It's defined by the people who built it, and the unspoken codes they share.

If you take the English to a desert island, in 100 years, you get Australia. If you take the Somalians to Sweden, in 100 years, you don't get another Sweden. You get something else entirely.

The Spanish colonised the Dominican Republic in 1493. Today it's a thriving country. West Africans were brought to Hispaniola in 1501. They overthrew their masters and became independent in 1791. Today, Haiti is one of the poorest nations in the world; the local delicacy is mud, and the average IQ is 67 [26].

This is why they don't care when schools no longer reflect the country in which they're located. This is why they cheer when native populations shrink, as long as GDP grows. This is why they view any resistance to demographic change as "backward" or "racist." Because in their eyes, everything is a market. And in a market, identity is irrelevant. All that matters is output. But identity isn't irrelevant. It's foundational.

I'm not advocating for ethno-nationalism. Identity is more than ethnicity. But at the same time, it would be absurd to pretend that ethnicity plays no role in identity for some nations, because for many countries, it clearly does. The Japanese. The Finns. The English. Their identity is rooted not just in civic paperwork or place, but in ancestry, history, and a deep sense of "us."

I could move to Vietnam, get a passport, marry a local, and have kids there. But would those kids be as Vietnamese as Ho Chi Minh? Obviously not. That doesn't mean they'd be unwelcome. It just means identity isn't fully transferable. It's not something you can download by filling out a form. Bureaucrats can't wave a magic wand and make me Vietnamese.

To illustrate this absurdity, just Google the French national football team in 1990, and then again in 2025. What changed? Did the millennia-old French ethnicity suddenly evolve more melanin? Of course not. They brought in more people from their former colonies, such as universities handing out scholarships to recruit athletes [27].

The jersey stays the same. The anthem plays. But the people beneath it have changed. The symbol remains, while the substance dissolves. That's the lie our rulers tell us: that nationality is a label, not a lineage. That culture is a moodboard. That home is just where you land. But identity isn't a costume. It's not granted. It's inherited. And when you sever the inheritance, you don't get a new nation. You get a husk that wears the old name.

This matters when building a nation that actually feels like home. Most people around the world understand this instinctively. No one calls it hateful for the Japanese to want Japan to remain Japanese. Or for the Igbo to speak of Igbo identity. Or for Hungarians to say Hungary belongs to Hungarians. Ethnic continuity is often seen as the norm — everywhere except among Europeans. Is the concept of an ethnic Magyar, Igbo, or Han evil? Or is it just the English, Irish, and French who aren't allowed to conceive of ourselves as an ethnos?

England is not just a patch of land, a set of values, or a fondness for tea. It is the inheritance of the English people. Without them, there is no England. No English, no England, no matter how seamless the so-called integration may be.

For the United States, ethnicity figures much less when it comes to identity. An actual nation of immigrants. What binds Americans is a shared story and a creed: the Constitution, the frontier spirit, the belief in freedom and self-reliance. It's mythos over bloodline. That's why it worked, for a time. But that system depended on assimilation. On people buying into the story. When that stops happening, America fractures.

This vision our leaders have is cold, soulless, and ultimately suicidal. A nation is not a company. Its citizens are not cogs. You cannot run a society like an Excel sheet. When you treat people like interchangeable economic units, don't be surprised when they stop feeling any loyalty to the place they live or the people around them.

What makes a country thrive is not cheap labour. It's shared values, trust, and identity. If identity is inherited, not downloaded, then history matters. Continuity matters. Lineage matters.

Which is why one of the most dishonest refrains in modern politics is the claim that "we're all a nation of immigrants." It's trotted out to dissolve borders, erase heritage, and shame anyone who resists demographic transformation. And it stuck, not because it's true in any meaningful sense, but because it's useful.

It became the story that justified everything. A tidy script for politicians, pundits, and bureaucrats to recite when the numbers didn't add up and the culture didn't fit. Trotted out as a conversation killer. Ah well, we're all from Africa anyway.

But myths like this don't just distort the present. They rewrite the past, and if left unchallenged, they will define the future.

4

Who Built the West?

My grandfather used to frequent Whitechapel. Business, friends, the odd drink, he knew the pubs, the norms, the people. It was rough in places, but it was English. Familiar. A neighbourhood with roots, where you could nod to faces on the corner and know they would nod back.

Today, it is something else entirely. A chaotic patchwork: run-down council estates, curry houses, bike lanes, cash and carry shops, students, charity clinics, drifting addicts, and a strong Bengali presence. Loud exhausts bounce off brick walls. Rubbish piles in doorways. Conversations shift languages mid-sentence. And behind it all, towering above the grime and disorder, the glass temples of Canary Wharf rise like a joke, global capital watching over a neighbourhood it long since abandoned.

And yet we are told by journalists, academics, and politicians that this is nothing new. That it has always been this way.

"We are a nation of immigrants."

It is the pseudo-intellectual mic drop meant to end all debate. But that line does not just rewrite the past; it insults the living memory of anyone who remembers otherwise.

Not a romantic myth. Not imperial nostalgia. Just lived experience. A generation ago, this place was something else. It had texture. Continuity. A shared story. That memory matters because not every nation is a nation of immigrants.

For some, the phrase fits better than others: the United States, Canada, Australia, and settler societies built on waves of arrival. But England is not. Ireland is not. Scotland is not. Germany is not. Finland is not. Sweden is not. Poland is not. Japan is not. China is not.

These are nations of ancestors. Nations of inheritance. Nations that existed before airports, passports, and "diversity" brochures. To erase that is not just dishonest. It is civilisational gaslighting.

These are rooted nations, culturally, historically, and ethnically. They were not built by global migration. They were built through continuity, myth, ancestry, and sacrifice. England, for example, has one of the most stable populations in the world. Genetic studies indicate that up to $73 \pm 4\%$ of Y chromosomes in early medieval English samples can be traced back to Bronze and Iron Age populations [28]. This is not a replacement. It is continuity.

"But what about the Huguenots?" asks the sherry-sipping, Waitrose-shopping, tweed-wearing middle-class bore. Yes, a few thousand French Protestants arrived in the 1600s. They were Christian, educated, Western. And crucially, they were few. A handful of European migrants four centuries ago does not mean we now owe open borders to the developing world.

Likewise, the fact that Europe saw tribal movements and wars in 1066 does not mean we are obligated to accept millions of low-skilled migrants today. History is not a blank cheque. Past invasions do not justify the present decline. You do not build immigration policy around medieval battles. You build it based on what your nation needs now.

Even in countries that were built by immigrants, like the U.S., Canada, and Australia, let us stop pretending it was some multicultural free-for-all. They were settled overwhelmingly by Western Europeans, particularly the British, who brought with them Enlightenment values, Christian traditions, the rule of law, democratic institutions, and a shared cultural foundation.

It was this civilisational core, not abstract diversity, that allowed pluralism to function at all.

And when others came, assimilation was not optional. In America, the expectation was crystal clear: renounce all prior allegiances, be of good moral character, and embrace American customs.

"We have room for but one flag, the American flag... We have room for but one language here, and that is the English language... and we have room for but one sole loyalty, and that is a loyalty to the American people." [29]

You changed your name. Your habits. Your food. Your faith, if needed. You became American, and nothing else. America was a melting pot. Immigrants were expected to melt.

Economically, it worked because there was no welfare state. If you came, you worked, or you starved. There were no handouts to exploit, no safety nets to game. Libertarian free movement only functions in a nation without a state dangling incentives.

That vision, cohesive, confident, demanding, is a far cry from what exists today.

Even the phrase itself, "nation of immigrants," is an American post-war invention. Not a founding truth, but a retroactive slogan used to rewrite the past and moralise the present. The Founders never saw themselves as immigrants. They saw the republic as a project rooted in shared ancestry and values, largely of Anglo-Protestant character.

"The consequences that must result from a too unqualified admission of foreigners... The safety of the republic depends essentially on the energy of a common National sentiment; on a uniformity of principles and habits; on the exemption of the citizens from foreign bias, and prejudice; and on that love of country which will almost invariably be found to be closely connected with birth, education, and family".

— Alexander Hamilton

Early immigration levels were modest, often consisting of just hundreds or a few thousand individuals per year. For generations, the nation expanded internally and consolidated its culture, rather than through open borders.

It was not until the late 19th century that immigration swelled, especially from Southern and Eastern Europe. With it came labour unrest, ideological radicalism, and rising social tension. The national response was swift: literacy tests, quotas, and, eventually, the 1924 Immigration Act, a moratorium designed to retain the country's cultural composition.

The "nation of immigrants" myth did not gain traction until much later. In 1958, the Anti-Defamation League commissioned Senator

John F. Kennedy to write an essay by that name, an effort to soften resistance to immigration and reframe the issue in moral terms. After his death, it was published as a book. The phrase entered the bloodstream of American political rhetoric, but only after the original nation had already begun to fade.

Then came 1965. The Hart–Celler Act dismantled the national origins system that had shaped immigration for over 40 years, a system designed to preserve the country's ethnic balance by heavily favouring immigrants from Northern and Western Europe while sharply limiting entries from other regions. Its architects promised it would not alter the country's ethnic makeup. They were wrong or dishonest. The new framework prioritised family reunification and skill categories, opening the gates to mass migration from the Global South.

In just two generations, the transformation has been profound. America has shifted from a culturally confident settler nation to a universalist state defined by pluralism, demographic churn, and the slow dissolution of shared identity.

And yet that one phrase, *"we are a nation of immigrants,"* is still repeated like gospel.

Being a nation of immigrants never meant being a borderless soup of clashing languages, religions, and values. It meant that some were invited, on the host nation's terms.

Today, the terms are gone.

Mass immigration now means everyone comes on their own terms. No expectation to adapt. No pressure to integrate. No concern for what it does to the host society.

Immigrants used to earn respect. They risked everything to come legally, to work hard, to start businesses, to live the American dream. But mass immigration, especially illegal immigration, destroyed that image. When your first act in a new country is breaking its laws, do not expect a hero's welcome. "Immigrant" no longer evokes the same sense of grit and gratitude. It evokes images of moochers, scammers, and a strain on the system.

Mass migration has done what no political argument could: it has turned once pro-immigration normies into sceptics. The shift in attitude did not come from ideology. It came from experience.

And even if you want to argue that a country was founded by immigrants, that does not mean it must accept endless immigration forever. It does not mean it has no right to say "enough." It does not mean it has no right to protect what it is.

Being a nation of immigrants is not a suicide pact.

And here is the kicker: only Western nations are ever told to forget who they are. Only we are expected to open our borders, abandon our traditions, and apologise for wanting to protect what is ours.

The hypocrisy is not subtle. It is the point.

And there is another lie, even more corrosive, woven into almost every modern discussion about immigration: that immigrants did not just arrive; they built Europe.

Immigrants did not build Britain. They did not build Sweden, France, or Germany. They came after the success. They came because these countries were already better, safer, freer, and fairer than the ones they left behind. They did not arrive with blueprints. They arrived with suitcases.

Take Britain. In 1951, there were only 30,000 people in the entire country who were not white. That is 0.07 percent of the population. This was after the Industrial Revolution, after the British Empire, after World War II. Britain had already invented modern democracy, built a global language, given the world Shakespeare and Newton, and launched the NHS. It was not migrants who made this happen. It was the British people.

We are told that immigration saved the NHS. But the NHS was launched in 1948. The Windrush ship arrived that same year, carrying fewer than 500 passengers. The idea that they built it is a historical fraud. Yes, some newcomers contributed. That is not the issue. The issue is that contribution is not the same as creation. Helping to maintain a house does not mean you laid its foundations. Replacing a lightbulb does not make you an architect.

And yet the myth is still pushed that Windrush was the birth of modern Britain. The country that built the world's biggest ever empire was apparently incapable of doing anything without some trainee bus conductors on HMS Windrush. That, without them, the country would have fallen apart. That is not only untrue, but also insulting. Insulting to the British working class who rebuilt the country after the Blitz. Insulting to the families who rationed, repaired, and endured. They did not need rescuing by anyone. They were the rescue.

Why can't Windrush simply be folded into a national story that does not absurdly inflate their role in a way that undercuts the broader population? Because it functions as retroactive legitimation for their open borders policy today. The same lie echoes across the continent.

Germans did not need Middle Eastern migrants in 2015 to build the Mercedes-Benz engine. The Swedes did not need Somali refugees to develop social democracy. France did not need Algerian migrants to write Voltaire, paint the Impressionists, or build the Eiffel Tower. Europe was not a blank slate waiting to be made whole by outsiders. It was already whole. Already exceptional.

"But what about colonialism?" they say. *"Europe got rich off exploitation."* More myth. More sleight of hand. The foundations of Western success — constitutional government, property rights, scientific inquiry, and free markets — were established long before the peak of imperialism. Britain's Industrial Revolution began in the 18th century, before most of its colonies had even been established. Germany, Japan, and Switzerland emerged as economic powerhouses with minimal colonial empires. Empire may have added extra, but it did not build the core. That came from within.

And if colonialism explains Europe's wealth, why did post-colonial nations not thrive in the same way after independence? Why is Haiti a failed state, while former British colonies like Australia and Canada became prosperous? Why did Singapore rise and Zimbabwe collapse?

The truth is simple. Europe built itself. And people came because of that. The migrant story is not a story of creation. It is a story of attraction. And now, somehow, we are being told that simply arriving in a prosperous country entitles you to claim credit for everything that came before. That you get to say "we" when talking about the NHS, or Oxford University, or the Royal Navy. No. You do not. You did not build it. You came after. You benefited from it. That is fine. But stop pretending you made it.

The lie matters because it erases the right of native populations to protect what they have built. If everyone built it, then everyone owns it. And if everyone owns it, no one can defend it. The entire moral foundation of national self-determination gets pulled out from under your feet.

And maybe that is the point. Because when you believe you built nothing, you believe you have no right to say no. But you did build something. You inherited something precious. And you are absolutely entitled to preserve it.

Let us be honest: immigrants can make significant contributions. Some did. Some do. But they did not build the West. And they certainly did not build Europe. Again, I am not saying immigrants never built anything in the West. As I have said, America is a nation of immigrants. But even in immigrant-built nations, timing and intent matter. There is a difference between those who helped build a country and those who arrived after the heavy lifting, only to critique and dismantle.

To our ruling class, national identity is not sacred. It is inconvenient, even threatening. And to make sure you never push back, they feed you another lie. They tell you that you built nothing. That everything you inherited, your safety, your freedom, your institutions, only exists because of the newcomers. That you owe them. That you should feel gratitude, not pride.

That immigrants were not just welcomed into these nations; they were always their backbone. That they built the roads, staffed the factories, created the institutions, and gave us prosperity. That without them, there would be no civilisation to preserve.

When it comes to Europe, it is nonsense. It is not just false. It is historically illiterate and morally perverse. A lie told often enough to obscure the truth and shame a population out of defending what it rightfully built. A claim that collapses the moment you look at the record.

And once you see that lie for what it is, another truth becomes clear. Only Western nations are told to accept this erasure, while every other culture guards its borders without apology.

5

Open Borders for Me, But Not for Thee

Everything you need to know about the immigration debate is summed up in one truth: immigration enforcement is only ever considered controversial when white-majority Western countries do it.

Non-Western nations enforce strict immigration laws without apology. Japan guards its homogeneity with pride, accepting fewer than 1 percent of asylum claims in 2022 [30]. Saudi Arabia doesn't grant citizenship to migrant workers. India, China, and Nigeria are not accused of xenophobia for protecting their borders or prioritising their people. These actions are seen as ordinary, unremarkable, and expected.

But when Western countries try to do the same, it's branded a moral crisis. Hungary and Poland are denounced as authoritarian for doing exactly what Japan does, and what most of the world takes for granted [31]. Yet those decisions have worked. Both countries remain safer, more stable, and more cohesive than many of their Western European neighbours. The media condemns, protesters organise, and international institutions pile on.

Only the West is expected to keep its doors open regardless of the cost. Try overstaying your visa in Japan; it won't involve a taxpayer-funded hotel or free dental. But in Britain, France, Germany, Canada, Australia, or the United States, you're expected to surrender your culture, your safety, and your identity, and smile while doing so.

This isn't global morality. It's ideological warfare targeted squarely at the West. What's under attack isn't the concept of borders, but the belief that Western nations have the right to say no. The right to decide who enters, who stays, and what kind of society they want to maintain.

Open borders are always for others. The same politicians who preach "no borders" live behind gates, hire private security, and send their kids to schools with admissions policies tighter than any visa regime. Even Parliament itself, the symbolic home of British democracy, is surrounded by a towering metal fence, ringed with CCTV and armed guards.

It isn't just hypocrisy. It's a theatre. Walls for them. Walls for their parties. Walls for their offices. Walls for their concerts. Just not for you.

In 2025, Glastonbury made the point almost too perfectly. From the stage, Jeremy Corbyn — the UK's ever-ridiculous Marxist MP — sermonised about a world without walls, leading chants of *build bridges, not walls* to a sea of cheering festival-goers. He and others spoke of tearing down fences, tearing up borders, and welcoming the world.

But every single person in that field had paid at least $400 for the privilege of being there, and all of them were standing safely behind a massive, expensive perimeter wall built around the festival grounds — a wall designed for one purpose only: to keep the uninvited out. The crowd applauded calls for "no borders" from inside a fortified enclosure they had paid to enter, blissfully unaware that they were living proof of the contradiction.

If this ideology were truly universal, we'd see the same pressure applied everywhere. But no one demands that China diversify. No one tells Saudi Arabia to open its borders. No one accuses Japan of racism for defending its cultural cohesion. Their sovereignty is respected.

What the technocrats and activists really want is for England to stop being English, France to stop being French, and Sweden to stop being Swedish. Cohesive Western nations aren't treated as models to emulate, but as problems to solve.

You see it plainly in how newcomers are allowed, sometimes even encouraged, to show open contempt for the very societies that welcomed them. Just think about it: people arrive by choice. They move into a stable, free, generous society, and immediately start lecturing the native population about how racist and backward they are. Or worse, they disregard social norms and commit crimes.

Imagine arriving at someone else's home and insulting the host while breaking their rules. Nowhere is this more obvious than in the case of Hamza Yousaf, the former First Minister of Scotland, who once stood in Parliament and bemoaned how *"white"* the country was, as if the historical demographics of Scotland were a moral failure.

Can you imagine moving to Pakistan and criticising it for being *"too brown"*? Of course not. You'd be run out of the country. And rightly so. Most people wouldn't dare behave that way abroad. And yet in the West, it's normal. Entire political movements, media narratives, and university departments are built on the routine denigration of native peoples. And still, we endure it. Quietly. Stoically.

The hostility isn't just internal. It's mirrored by the global hypocrisy that only targets Western nations. If this were about compassion, we'd see campaigns urging Beijing to resettle 100,000 Rohingya Muslims. If it were about equity, we'd see pressure on Ghana to take in Syrian refugees. But no such demands exist. Because it was never about diversity. It was about dissolving the West and calling it progress.

Western nations erase their traditions, appease hostile ideologies, and sacrifice coherence at the altar of tolerance. We tell ourselves it's compassion, it's progress. But the truth is darker. The altruism of the West may be the very thing that brings it down.

If you enjoy traveling to Vietnam for authentic pho, or to Morocco to wander the souks, or to Namibia to witness intact tribal customs, then you should oppose mass migration. The same logic applies to England, to France, to Finland. Culture only survives when it is rooted, protected, and allowed to flourish in its own soil.

People seem to recognise that cultural homogeneity is desirable, at least when they go on holiday. That's the whole point of travel: to experience somewhere with a distinct identity. We instinctively value cultural cohesion when we're tourists. Yet we're told it's backward or bigoted to want the same thing at home.

Mass migration doesn't spread culture. It dilutes it. It erases it. Until everywhere feels like nowhere. That charming stretch of southern France that tourists adore for being "so typically French"? They vote for the far right, not out of hate, but because they don't want to stop being French.

And the most dangerous double standard lies not only in how borders are policed, but in what the West is importing — not just people, but worldviews. Belief systems that openly contradict the values we claim to stand for, yet are welcomed and defended in the name of tolerance.

Nowhere is this more apparent than in the alliance between progressives and the most regressive major ideology on Earth: Islam. This is the culture now being imported, on a massive scale, into Europe and North America.

By every metric, Islam stands in stark opposition to the principles progressives claim to uphold: gender equality, gay rights, secular law, and freedom of speech. And yet, Islam is protected. Criticising it is taboo. Challenging it is considered hate speech.

This contradiction isn't accidental; it's enforced. The term *"Islamophobia"* is increasingly used not to protect Muslims from violence, but to preserve an ideology from scrutiny.

"A word created by fascists, and used by cowards, to manipulate morons."

— Christopher Hitchens

You can mock Christianity, deride Western history, attack the family, the nation, the flag, but question a set of ideas tied to Islam, and you're suddenly dangerous. Islam doesn't spread through coexistence. It spreads through control.

In Canada, Adil Charkaoui, a frequent public speaker in Montreal, openly declares things like "Kill the Zionist aggressors" and praises Islamist terrorists as the "good guys." Montreal shrugs. Then Sean Feucht visits — a Christian singer who sings about love and peace —

and he's treated as a pariah. In this upside-down moral order, the preacher of violence is tolerated, and the singer of hymns is cast out.

Today in Britain, Christian preachers are arrested while calls to Islamic prayer echo from public loudspeakers. The native tradition bends. The foreign one asserts.

Muslims make up just 6.5 percent of the UK population [32], yet account for 90 percent of terror-related deaths since 2000 [33], 75 percent of active terror threats [34], and 18 percent of the prison population [35]. They are linked to 84 percent of gang-based child sexual exploitation cases [36]. Only one in four British Muslims believes Hamas committed murder and rape in Israel on October 7 [37]. There are an estimated 6,000 cases of female genital mutilation each year in the UK [38], and children born in these communities face a 50 percent higher rate of birth defects [39].

France banned full-face coverings in 2011 [40]. Denmark followed in 2018 [41], and in 2025 proposed extending that ban to schools and universities [42]. The Netherlands has restricted them in hospitals, on public transport, and in classrooms [43].

This is not "Islamophobic." It was civilisational self-respect. In liberal societies, you cannot build a high-trust democracy when half the population is told to vanish from view.

But perhaps the most disturbing part is how little public opinion mattered. Mass migration didn't result from public demand. It was imposed from above. Even Brexit, the most apparent democratic demand, resulted in record-high immigration [44], and the political class carried on as usual.

When democratic resistance emerges, whether through protest, referendum, or the election of populist candidates, it's not respected. It's smeared. For decades, working Americans have watched their country transform, demographically, culturally, and politically, without their consent. Conservatives offered up centrist Republicans like Mitt Romney, tried to play by the rules, sought compromise, and were mocked for it. Meanwhile, the borders stayed open, their neighbourhoods changed overnight, their kids faced discrimination under DEI and affirmative action, and every attempt to speak up was met with accusations of far-right zealotry.

Even the path to opportunity was quietly closed off. As Marc Andreessen recently noted, *"If you're a smart kid from rural Wisconsin, you're fooling yourself if you think you'll get into a top university."* At Columbia, over half of the students are now foreign nationals. Across the Ivy League, international enrollment has soared from single digits to 30%, 40%, even 50%, while DEI policies further tilt the scales against white and white middle-class kids. The meritocracy they were promised no longer exists. It was replaced by imported student cash cows and ideological filters. That's an incredible betrayal. American schools should obviously prioritise American students.

Trump wasn't the start of the radicalisation of working Americans. He was a response to it. And even that response was met with impeachments, investigations, and political prosecutions. Under Biden, things only escalated: inflation, mass illegal crossings, collapsing norms, and what many see as the state turning openly hostile to dissent. When even assassination attempts are brushed aside, the message becomes clear. This is no longer a conversation. Their patience has run out.

In that context, the desire for an America First policy, mass deportation, reindustrialisation, and a reassertion of national sovereignty is entirely understandable. And of course, the global intelligentsia hates it. Because it says what they fear most: that the era of polite surrender in America is over. Because it signals to the rest of the world that you can reject the ideology of open borders and mass migration and not only survive, but thrive.

Which is exactly why it must be crushed. Not debated. Defeated. The ruling class sees nationalism not as disagreement, but as rebellion. And they treat rebellion the only way tyrannies ever do: with suppression.

When a culture is told for long enough that its borders are immoral, that its history is shameful, and that its identity is negotiable, it begins to hollow out. The foundations weaken first, almost imperceptibly, and then—one day—they give way.

6

The Anatomy of Collapse

C ivilisations don't fall in a day. They fall the way a mountain erodes, slowly, silently, then all at once. Sometimes they're destroyed by invasion or catastrophe. But more often, they collapse from within. Not because of foreign enemies at the gate, but because of rot at the core. Because they forget who they are. Because they trade identity for convenience, and borders for virtue.

Rome didn't collapse because the Visigoths were uniquely strong. It collapsed because Rome stopped believing in Rome. It invited wave after wave of migrants, some claiming asylum, others bringing chaos, and told itself it was being noble. But these groups never assimilated. They remained loyal to the tribe, not to the empire. Roman elites outsourced their own defence to mercenaries with no stake in the nation's future. Citizenship was cheapened. Traditions faded. And when the barbarians finally walked through the gates, there was no one left willing to fight for what remained.

As Christopher Hitchens once warned:

"The barbarian never takes the city until someone holds the gates open for them. And it's your own preachers and multicultural authorities who'll do it for you... resist, resist it while you can."

The enemies of a civilisation rarely need to breach its walls. They wait until someone inside unlatches the doors. Civilisational collapse is never purely an external event; it's an inside job. A betrayal dressed as compassion. A suicide performed in the name of virtue. Not by foreign invaders with swords, but by domestic elites with slogans.

Sound familiar?

We spoke earlier about suicidal empathy, that uniquely Western instinct to prioritise the feelings of outsiders over the fate of insiders. This is it in action. It confuses openness with strength, surrender with grace. And it leads otherwise intelligent societies to lower their defences, invite in dysfunction, and call it moral progress.

The result isn't just disorder. It's dilution. A slow unravelling of the cultural core until what's left is unrecognisable. History offers no shortage of warnings.

The Abbasid Caliphate followed a similar arc. As the Islamic Empire grew rich, it filled its institutions with outsiders — Turkic soldiers and Persian bureaucrats — until the caliphs became figureheads, and the empire fractured into competing interests. When the Mongols finally arrived in 1258, Baghdad collapsed almost effortlessly. The structure was still there. The soul was gone.

Modern Lebanon offers a recent warning. Once a Christian majority nation called the "Switzerland of the Middle East," it opened its doors to waves of Palestinian and later Syrian migrants. The demographic balance shifted. Sectarian conflict followed. Today, Lebanon is a failed state — its capital ruled by militias, its economy shattered, its culture divided beyond repair. [45][46].

Meanwhile, the strongest societies in history didn't thrive on diversity or fluid identity. They thrived on clarity, cohesion, and conviction.

Sparta built an entire warrior culture on loyalty to tribe and tradition. Foreigners were not absorbed; they were distrusted. Every male citizen was trained from childhood to fight and die for the collective. Cowardice was a crime. Conformity to shared values wasn't oppressive; it was the price of survival.

The Mongols forged the largest contiguous empire in history, not by tolerance or inclusion, but through unity of purpose. Loyalty to the Khan. One code. One law. Outsiders could live, but never lead.

In Japan, the samurai class played a pivotal role in shaping a society characterised by discipline, ritual, and honour. Feudal Japan wasn't multicultural. It was deliberately insular. Under the Tokugawa shogunate, the country sealed itself off from the world for over 200 years through a policy known as *sakoku* — not out of fear, but out of a desire for cultural preservation. Foreigners were banned. Christianity was outlawed. Trade was tightly controlled. Japan didn't open its borders until it was forced to at gunpoint by the American Commodore Perry in 1853. And even then, it opened reluctantly, cautiously, without compromising national identity.

Imperial China offers another example. For thousands of years, it was held together not just by dynastic rule, but by a coherent civilisational identity: Confucian values, ancestor worship, shared language, and rites. Foreigners were often kept at the edges, sometimes even welcomed, but they were expected to assimilate. "Barbarians" could trade, sometimes serve, but China remained the center of its own world.

Even the modern West, at its peak, understood this. The Britain that defeated the Nazis wasn't a "post-national" experiment. The America that built the Apollo program didn't run on TikTok identity politics. These were confident, high-trust nations. They knew who they were and expected anyone who joined to earn their place.

Now we've flipped the formula. We allow millions in from alien cultures. We demand nothing in return. And when that predictably breeds conflict, we call it progress. This is how you become a third-world country: when immigration erodes any sense of shared interest, and people are asked to sacrifice for the good of others who aren't them — and who won't return the favour.

A nation that forgets itself becomes a border, not a home. And when that happens, collapse isn't a question of if, only when.

And yet, this unravelling isn't just ignored. It's celebrated. Rebranded as progress. We're told that fragmentation is a strength. That the loss of identity is inclusion. That importing endless differences will somehow create unity.

It's an experiment at best, and a boldfaced lie at worst.

7

Diversity is Not a Strength

We've been sold a lie that importing millions of people from radically different cultures will somehow make us stronger. That every new language, every new religion, every new worldview added to the mix will magically create harmony. We're told *"diversity is our strength."* It's a dogma that can't be questioned. Airhead politicians like Justin Trudeau bleat it like wind-up dolls, but never actually explain how.

Yet, before "diversity made us stronger," we had lower crime rates, better wages, affordable housing, solid healthcare, good schools, no integration chaos, no obsession with race, national confidence, and grooming meant personal hygiene.

Diversity is our strength is Orwellian doublespeak. Diversity, by definition, means difference. And difference, at scale, means division. No team wins disunited. No family thrives without shared values. No civilisation holds when it speaks in fifty tongues and believes in none.

Take Iceland. One of the most peaceful, prosperous, and safe countries on Earth. Virtually no crime. A strong, cohesive society built on deep-rooted trust, homogeneity, and a shared culture that stretches back over a thousand years. It ranks at the top of the Global Peace Index year after year [47]. It works not in spite of its lack of diversity, but because of it.

England once had this too: an instinctive civility, a shared rhythm of life, the dignity of familiarity. Not a utopia, but a home. A country of orderly queues, dry humour, and quiet pride. Strength comes from unity, shared identity, and coherence, from people pulling in the same direction. That used to be obvious. But in the modern West, up is down. Borders are bigotry. Dissent is hate. And the more fractured we become, the more we're told we should feel empowered. It's nonsense. The truth is simple: unity is strength. Diversity, without assimilation, is entropy.

Ask yourself, if diversity is such a superpower, why isn't China, our biggest global competitor, actively pursuing it too? Why aren't they importing millions from the world's poorest, most unstable regions to compete with our "diversity"? Why do they avoid Islam like the plague? Why aren't they issuing H1B-style visas to half of India? Why are they doing the exact opposite? Because it's not a superpower, it's a liability. And they know it [48].

Mass migration on a large scale creates segregated enclaves with their own languages, laws, and allegiances. Think Sweden's no-go zones or France's banlieues, mini Islamist strongholds where the state has effectively ceded control. In places like Molenbeek in Belgium or the outskirts of Paris, gangs run the streets, drug money fuels the underground economy, and radical imams preach jihad with impunity. Police won't go in. Journalists are attacked. Sharia, not secular law, fills the vacuum [49].

As one French Algerian teenager told *Libération* in 2018:

"I live in France, but I'm not French. I'm Muslim. We have our own rules."

That's not integration. That's a soft partition. And it's spreading [50].

In the UK, entire boroughs have begun to operate as de facto enclaves. In Tower Hamlets, multiple investigations have uncovered extremist-linked school boards and cases where women were told to cover their heads to access public services. In 2015, a *Times* investigation found that sharia councils were operating unofficially, issuing rulings on marriage and custody, often in direct contradiction to British law [51].

Which Western city has improved as a result of large-scale Muslim immigration? London? Amsterdam? Paris? New York? None. They've all gotten worse. More fractured, more dangerous, more tense. The promise was harmony. The result is division, decay, and decline. You can't have a cohesive nation when millions of people live in parallel cultures [52].

At the core of any prosperous nation is social capital: the trust between neighbours, the shared rules, the sense of mutual belonging. Mass migration wrecks that. You don't trust the people around you because they don't behave like you. You don't know your neighbours. You stop volunteering. You hunker down. In high-trust societies, people often leave their doors unlocked. In low-trust ones, you build fences and hope they hold.

Everything good in a society flows from trust and cohesion. That stability isn't conjured by slogans or government programs; it's built from the ground up. Strong families raise responsible citizens. Strong industries generate the wealth to fund public goods. Together they anchor local communities, creating the framework for a nation people believe in.

Harvard professor Robert Putnam demonstrated this in his research: greater diversity is associated with lower trust [53]. Not just between groups, but within them too. So instead of a warm, united community, you get fragmented enclaves full of suspicion, withdrawal, and resentment [54].

You can feel the collapse of social trust in Western cities: locked public restrooms, surveillance cameras on every corner, and even Starbucks is taking out the chairs inside. One mark of a healthy society is how we expect people to behave when nobody's watching, and by that measure, we've fallen.

You can see it in places built for community, such as parks, schools, and the high street. There are two parks we take our kids to. One is located in a nice neighbourhood, but it is flanked by two housing towers with a heavy immigrant population. The other is further out, with no towers and no settlement blocks. Guess which park has music blasting from Bluetooth speakers? Guess which one has toys left in the sandpit, untouched and waiting for any child to play with? You already know.

It's the same story with schools. Middle-class parents talk endlessly about "fit," "values," and "Ofsted ratings." They'll say the school just didn't feel right. That little Hugo "wasn't thriving." But what they won't say, what they can't say, is that they didn't want to send their kid to a school where specific demographics are overrepresented. Where the culture feels foreign. They don't say it at book club. Or brunch. Or on WhatsApp. But they all act on it anyway. Everyone knows. No one says it.

You see the fracturing in the calendar, in the rituals that once stitched a people together. What used to feel like a shared narrative now feels like competing broadcasts. I remember when public rituals meant something. When they brought people together, not because of where they came from, but because of where they were. Shared place. Shared story.

Remembrance Sunday used to feel sacred. A whole country pausing. Poppies on lapels. Heads bowed. A shared moment of gratitude. Now, in parts of London, it barely registers. Some schools don't mark it. In certain boroughs, wearing a poppy earns you hostility. I've seen people talk through the silence. Last year, pro-Palestine chants echoed through central London the same weekend thousands gathered to honour the dead. The war heroes being remembered aren't "ours" anymore. The memory no longer binds.

And then there's St George's Day. England's national day, if you can still call it that. You'd be forgiven for not noticing it. No flags. No fanfare. Celebrating it is treated as vaguely shameful, maybe even racist. Meanwhile, Diwali lights up Trafalgar Square. Eid gets parades and funding. Black History Month fills the calendar. The new rule is simple: in the name of inclusion, everything is celebrated except the culture that built the country.

This is what "diversity" means in practice. Not peaceful coexistence. Not mutual enrichment. Just a quiet replacement. Rituals that once made you feel part of something bigger now remind you that you're being pushed out. The new festivals don't include you. And the old ones are quietly erased.

When a culture shifts from shared norms to imported ones, everyday life degrades. The UK is now locking up steaks and Red Bull cans in grocery stores, not because of war or famine, but because social trust is collapsing, one anti-theft tag at a time.

Migration advocates cling to the idea of universal human sameness, the belief that deep down, we're all the same. That every society is equally valid, equally functional, equally good. It's a colossal denial of history, language, and civilisational difference. The people arriving are not blank slates. They are products of radically different histories, often histories that are indifferent or even hostile to ours. They do not arrive value-free. They bring their own values, shaped elsewhere, and often incompatible with or corrosive to the values we hold dear. We've bought into the myth of universality, the idea that all peoples, all norms, all ways of life are interchangeable. Ironically, it was Western achievement and egalitarianism that enabled this belief. And in embracing it, we've eroded our own cultural confidence, leaving ourselves wide open to the quiet conquest of alien values.

Once one of the most LGBT-friendly cities on Earth, London is now among the most homophobic. Why? Because entire boroughs are dominated by ultra-conservative migrant communities who openly reject Western views on sexuality. In some areas, being openly gay is downright dangerous. We spent decades fighting for tolerance, only to import people who want to dismantle it. We imported intolerance, then got scolded for noticing it.

We're now dealing with deep-rooted misogyny, tribalism, and medieval worldviews:

- Cousin marriage leading to birth defects
- Honour killings
- Acid attacks
- Forced marriage
- Female genital mutilation
- Blasphemy laws enforced with threats of violence
- Animal torture (halal) to satisfy alien religious doctrine

In Pakistan, approximately 66 percent of marriages involve blood relatives [55]. Among British Pakistanis, around 55 percent are between first cousins [56]. In Bradford, a high Pakistani city, 60 percent of children born between 2007 and 2011 had first-cousin parents [57]. This practice is taboo in the West and a public health disaster. Children face higher risks of genetic disorders, developmental issues, and chronic illness. A 2013 report by Professor Alan Bittles estimated that the NHS spends over £100 million annually dealing with these cases [58]. And yet, tribal voting blocs push back against banning the practice, citing racism. Mainstream politicians are too scared to act.

The UK is now seeing a decline in average IQ for the first time in recorded history [59]. A nation's future depends on its cognitive capital, its ability to produce inventors, engineers, scientists, and leaders. Yet we're importing people from countries with lower average cognitive outcomes, often shaped by cultures that reinforce these deficits. It is a fact that inbreeding impacts IQ negatively, and the data show that these gaps persist across generations, not diminishing over time.

On a British-based matchmaking platform called Nikkahgram, Muslim men are explicitly encouraged to seek "a shy, untouched spouse" and take on second, third, or fourth wives, with polygyny framed as the righteous Islamic solution. Virgin women under 35 are marketed as "high quality" first wife material. In contrast, older women or those with any sexual history are compared to "low quality products," whose only option is to share a husband. The site promotes itself as "the definitive Nikkah service for those rare Muslims who still value" these traits, an outlook fundamentally at odds with Western values of gender equality, individual dignity, and monogamous partnership. It also features Dr. Asif Munaf, a suspended medic known for antisemitic remarks, who uses his medical title to lend credibility to misogynistic claims, including that women have a "deficiency in their intellect." This is not cultural diversity. It is the normalisation of a worldview that undermines the social and moral foundations of the society in which it is hosted.

In parts of Belgium, the UK, and France, Sharia law governs daily life. Women are pressured into hijabs. Apostates are threatened. Property disputes are settled in illegal religious courts. What was once the cradle of common law now tolerates parallel legal systems rooted in medieval doctrine. These aren't fringe practices. They're widespread and growing [60].

Immigration doesn't end at the border. There's a second wave, a migration into institutions, such as schools, city halls, police forces, and media boards. And as these institutions change hands, so do the values they uphold. What was once built on shared norms becomes fragmented. The culture shifts, and with it, the logic of politics.

Mass migration doesn't just change how people live. It changes how they vote. In high-trust societies, politics is about ideas. In balkanised ones, it becomes tribal. It's no longer about the common good; it's about what your group can extract.

As Lee Kuan Yew warned:

"In multiracial societies, you don't vote in accordance with your economic interests, you vote in accordance with race and religion." [61]

As immigrants and their descendants grow into a larger share of the electorate, their political preferences begin to reshape the direction of entire nations. And what people need to understand is that in many ways, legal immigration from the Third World poses a far greater long-term threat than illegal immigration ever could. Illegal migrants can be deported. Legal ones settle, gain voting power, and reshape the political landscape. They move into your cities, vote in their co ethnics, and over time, the institutions begin to reflect the values of their homelands rather than yours.

You don't get law and order. You get tribal politics and corruption.

Look at the UK. The grooming gangs didn't appear out of nowhere. They were protected by local authorities, often immigrant politicians who were voted into office by entirely legal, law-abiding immigrants brought over decades ago to work in factories [62].

Westerners take for granted how rare non-tribal political culture is. In much of the world, elections are often reduced to simple ethnic headcounts. Loyalty flows through kinship, not principle. The West's trust in rules and the common good was a civilisational advantage. But that openness now leaves us exposed. Import tribalism at scale, and civic democracy becomes a spoils system [63].

In 2023, British MPs were lobbying for a new airport in Mirpur, Pakistan. Not to boost British trade or tourism. Not for diplomatic reasons. But because large swathes of the British Pakistani population, especially in places like Luton, Bradford, and Birmingham, trace their roots back to that region. Mirpur, by the way, is one of the most backward areas in Pakistan. Tribalism runs deep. Cousin marriage is the norm. Political life revolves around clan loyalty, not civic principle. And that same mindset has been imported into Britain, along with the population. So when Mirpuri voters elect their man to Parliament, they expect him to deliver — not for Britain, but for the biraderi.

This is what happens when identity politics is built around imported notions of identity. A British MP becomes a mouthpiece for a village in Pakistan. Foreign interests override national ones. And the rest of the country is expected to pretend this is normal [64].

In cities like Brussels, the socialist vote neatly overlaps with neighbourhoods populated by immigrants from Turkey, Morocco, and sub-Saharan Africa. These groups overwhelmingly support parties that promise expanded welfare, amnesty, and state intervention, policies that offer them direct material benefit [65].

In Denmark, the second most popular party among Muslim voters is the Red-Green Alliance. This far-left faction wants to dismantle capitalism entirely and put firms and property under state control. Even by Danish standards, it is extreme, yet it is gaining ground because it speaks to the interests of a new, growing voting bloc [66].

This creates a political ratchet: the more migrants arrive, the more votes flow to parties that promise more migration and more redistribution. Over time, the founding population can find itself outnumbered, outvoted, and politically sidelined in the countries their ancestors built.

The result is not just higher taxes or expanding welfare. It is a permanent shift in the national character and the rules of the game.

Immigration, in this light, is not just a demographic or cultural issue. It becomes a slow, democratic transfer of power, away from the native population and toward groups with entirely different values, visions, and loyalties [67].

In Britain, ethnic and religious blocs vote almost monolithically. The most unsettling realisation comes not from new arrivals, but from second- and third-generation immigrants who still identify more with the tribal politics of their ancestral homelands. When British MPs signal allegiance to foreign causes or movements like Hamas, it raises fundamental questions about loyalty, integration, and the viability of multicultural democracy.

If citizenship no longer requires a shared cultural and moral foundation, then governance devolves into ethnic bloc voting [68].

In the U.S., identity politics has overtaken ideas. At a certain point, diversity overwhelms democracy, because people stop voting for ideas and start voting for their tribe.

In New York City, Zohran Mamdani, a socialist, pro-Palestinian activist, and anti-capitalist, was elected in a district reshaped by mass immigration. He identifies as Indian and Ugandan, immigrated seven years ago, and now holds power in one of the world's most influential cities [69].

And he's not an outlier. Mass immigration has seeded ideological shifts that are now flowering into real political power. The U.S. imported anti-Americanism, cultivated it in schools, and now reaps the crop.

Take Minnesota. Minneapolis is home to one of the largest Somali populations outside Africa. In Ilhan Omar's district, Somalis vote nearly unanimously, not on policy, but identity. This bloc voting gives them immense political power, despite persistent reports of ballot harvesting, clan-based campaigning, and voter intimidation [70].

State Senator Omar Fateh, a self-described socialist, recently won the Democratic endorsement for mayor of Minneapolis over the sitting mayor, Jacob Frey. His brother-in-law, Muse Mohamed, pleaded the Fifth before the state Senate Ethics Committee over a ballot harvesting scheme, one in which federal investigators confirmed he had illegally handled ballots.

A textbook example of low-trust culture behaviour.

Fateh avoided direct consequences, but was still sanctioned for failing to disclose campaign payments. As a legislator, he's backed some of the most radical proposals in the state, including free or reduced healthcare for illegal immigrants. He aims to leverage government power to benefit his Somali community.

And as we'll see later, that same community is responsible for a staggering share of crime in Minnesota.

In fact, it's pretty challenging to discern what the U.S. has gained by incorporating this community into its melting pot. Somalia and the United States occupy opposite ends of nearly every developmental measure. The average IQ in Somalia is 67, compared to 100 in the U.S. Over 60 percent of Somalis are illiterate. In the U.S., that figure is 18 percent. And while the U.S. birth rate has collapsed to 1.6 per woman, Somalia's stands at a staggering 6.2 [71].

It's not difficult to see where this is going. These aren't just cultural quirks. They are generational fault lines in intelligence, literacy, income, and fertility. Yet mass migration policy pretends these differences don't matter, as if importing a nation into another won't transform it. As if Minneapolis isn't already being reshaped by this influx — the norms, institutions, and the very character of the city itself.

Across Europe, ethnic and religious parties now openly cater to migrant communities. In the Netherlands, DENK campaigns almost entirely on pro migrant platforms. In Belgium, the Islamic Party wants Sharia law [72].

In the UK, Pakistani and Bangladeshi enclaves like Bradford and Tower Hamlets elect Muslim mayors and MPs who campaign on sectarian issues. In Tower Hamlets, Lutfur Rahman, who was removed for fraud, was re-elected in 2022 with overwhelming ethnic support. Not merit. Not reform. Pure ethnic solidarity.

In Birmingham, a councillor campaigns against men and women "mixing freely" in Britain in 2025. A Labour MP calls for an Islamic blasphemy law [73].

In Canada, entire ridings swing on diaspora loyalties. In places like Scarborough, Mississauga, and Vancouver East, political parties campaign in languages such as Punjabi, Mandarin, and Urdu. Candidates are selected from within ethnic communities and are promised targeted benefits. It's not civic politics. It's vote buying by demographic segmentation [74].

In 2023, a Brampton parade featured a float celebrating the assassination of Indian PM Indira Gandhi, re-enacted with papier mâché rifles and bloodied effigies. The organisers weren't underground radicals. They were part of a growing, influential Khalistani separatist movement operating openly across Ontario and B.C. [75].

That same year, after the killing of Hardeep Singh Nijjar, an alleged terrorist, Khalistani mobs doxxed Hindu Canadian leaders, vandalised temples, and threatened journalists. Posters in Canadian cities labelled Indian diplomats as "killers" [76].

What should've been a foreign policy issue became a domestic riot risk.

Canada is now seeing the emergence of parallel political blocs, weaponised by transnational loyalties. Somali MPs campaign by clan. Chinese diaspora groups are accused of election interference. Tamil activists lobby for Sri Lankan territory. Muslim groups rally for foreign insurgencies. Palestinian and Israeli supporters turn Canadian streets into ideological warzones.

None of this strengthens national unity. It fractures it.

It pulls people away from a shared identity and into imported tribalism.

This kind of multiculturalism didn't erase tribalism. It gave it a passport and a vote [77].

What you're seeing isn't democracy. It's sectarian politics, Balkan style. The nation dissolves into voting blocs. Trust collapses. Elections become a census [78].

And here's the bitter irony: even as our cities fracture and our politics tribalise, we're told to shut up and celebrate it. To keep waving the *"diversity is our strength"* banner while the ground crumbles beneath us.

Yet across the world, other nations do the exact opposite. They protect their cultural integrity without apology, and no one calls them hateful.

Japan isn't called racist for preserving its culture. Bhutan tightly controls migration. Dubai gives preference to native citizens, and nobody complains.

But when the Irish say Ireland is for the Irish, or when the English say England is for the English?

Suddenly, it's hate.

You don't have to apologise for wanting your country to remain your country. Because the more divided we become, the more expensive the illusion gets.

Diversity doesn't just erode trust. It inflates the cost. Social programs strain. Infrastructure buckles. Schools, hospitals, housing — all stretched to serve a population that no longer shares a center.

So if you won't defend your culture for moral reasons, fine. But take a look at the bill.

Because the cracks aren't just showing. They're spreading, through every sector, every system, every spreadsheet.

8

The Economic Cost of Mass Migration

Mass migration is often sold as an economic win. "Migrants grow the economy," we're told by politicians chasing stats and corporations chasing margins. And yes, importing more people can increase total economic output. But it also dilutes the pie. The real question is, who gets a bigger slice? Because when wages stagnate, rents explode, and public services buckle, that "growth" means nothing to the average citizen.

The political class, along with groups like the IMF, World Bank, and Cato Institute, all point to GDP as the scoreboard. But GDP isn't wealth. It's output. And what actually shapes living standards is output per person, GDP per capita. Even that has limits. GDP is a poor measure of a society's actual well-being. It says nothing about whether people can thrive.

A country can have a rising GDP while housing becomes unaffordable, wages flatline, public services collapse, crime rises, and mental health deteriorates. Meanwhile, what people actually care about is whether their kids will be able to buy a home by the time they're 30.

Whether the streets are safe. Whether schools are decent, jobs are meaningful, and doctors are accessible without waiting years.

GDP counts war, disease, and rebuilding after disaster as economic positives, because money changes hands. But it doesn't tell you if your nation is liveable, fair, or united. It doesn't measure cohesion. A healthy society isn't just productive; it's also resilient. It's one that works, one people want to stay in, contribute to, and pass on.

In 2023, Canada's GDP hit record highs. So did the food bank use. Homelessness. Wages dropped. Housing soared. Hospitals overflowed. GDP grew, but Canadians got poorer [79]. A country can double its GDP by doubling its population, but if quality of life collapses in the process, what is being gained? Not much. The only people who benefit from this are those at the top: the politicians who boast about growth, the corporations that enjoy low-cost workers, the bureaucrats whose budgets swell, and the new arrivals who receive free benefits.

For ordinary citizens, the measure of success isn't abstract output. It's concrete well-being. We don't want a bigger pie. We want a bigger slice. And when migration floods the labour market, it erodes that slice, shrinking wages and stretching resources.

A labour shortage isn't a crisis. It's an opportunity. It forces employers to raise wages, invest in productivity, and treat workers better. After the Black Death wiped out up to half of Scotland's population, wages for peasants tripled. Today's elites would panic. They'd yell, *"Quick, fly in a million Somalis!"* But medieval Scotland had no Ryanair, and the people rebuilt with what they had.

Ironically, it wasn't long ago that the Left understood the economic downside of mass immigration. Bernie Sanders once called open borders a *"Koch brothers idea,"* warning that flooding the labour market would *"make everybody in America poorer"* [80]. Paul Collier, a respected Oxford economist, argued that mass migration *"harms social cohesion and drives inequality"* [81]. Harvard's George Borjas, the leading expert on immigration economics, found that low-skilled immigration depresses native wages, particularly for those without a degree [82].

Borjas found that a 10 percent increase in the labour force driven by immigrants reduces native wages in competing sectors by 3 to 4 percent [83]. The National Academies of Sciences confirmed that first-generation immigrants cost governments more than they contribute over their lifetimes [84]. Even the OECD admits that over 75 percent of recent migrants to Europe are low-skilled, despite the popular narrative about engineers and doctors, and are disproportionately reliant on public services [85].

In 1973, shortly before his death, French President Georges Pompidou admitted that he opened the immigration floodgates at the request of prominent businessmen. Their goal was to suppress French wages and break up the labour movement.

So who actually benefits from this "growth"? Not the working class. Not the taxpayer. Not the nurse whose hospital is overwhelmed. It's the corporation that gets cheaper labour. The landlord who profits from scarcity. The politician who secures a new voting bloc. This isn't economic policy. It's a pyramid scheme. And eventually, someone gets left holding the bill.

While economists theorise, ordinary families pay the price. Kids losing scholarships to newcomers who tick the right boxes. Teen jobs are disappearing, being handed to adult migrants working on student visas. Homes become unaffordable. What's the message to native born children? That merit doesn't matter. That their own country has no loyalty to them. That fairness now means exclusion.

People are growing tired of always being last in line. Tired of watching their taxes fund benefits they're barred from. Of being told to wait, work harder, sacrifice, while newcomers leapfrog the queue, get housed faster, treated faster, handed more, and expected less. It's not just a perception anymore. It's a draining reality: you pay in, they take out. You follow the rules, they rewrite them. And your kids grow up thinking this is normal.

In the UK, the Office for Budget Responsibility confirms that low-wage migrants typically never repay the cost of the public services they consume. According to OECD data, over 75 percent of immigrants to Europe in the past decade were low-skilled, contrary to popular narratives that often focus on doctors and engineers [85]. A landmark study by University College London found that non-European migrants cost the UK £120 billion between 1995 and 2011 [86].

Today, the fiscal burden continues to grow. Households with at least one foreign national now claim nearly £1 billion per month in welfare, double the amount from just three years ago [87]. Meanwhile, the government spends over £100 million each month housing asylum seekers in hotels, a figure often exaggerated but still staggering in scale [88].

Walk through any small town in Britain and you'll see where that money is going: groups of young, able-bodied foreign men, not working or integrating, but loitering - a visible sign of a system stretched to its limit.

Asylum seekers are increasingly prioritised for social housing, placed ahead of British citizens who have been waiting for years, including struggling families and our own homeless veterans. Councils, under pressure from central mandates and legal obligations, hand over limited housing stock to recent arrivals while locals remain trapped on waiting lists. Many of these migrants, even when their claims are rejected, cannot be deported, protected by layers of NGO advocacy and humanitarian law.

And now, in reaction to locals protesting against hotels being filled with migrants, the government is taking it further: paying councils to buy up homes with British taxpayers' money — only to lease them back to the Home Office to house asylum seekers, not the British people. Total madness.

Londoners now pay an average of £216 more in monthly rent due to immigration-driven demand, and nearly 48 percent of all social housing in London is occupied by foreign-born residents. Far from the image of net contributors and economic saviors, Britain's immigration reality is one of long-term dependency, mounting public costs, and a political class too cowardly to course correct.

Muslims in the UK — 80.2 percent of working-age adults do not work. Only 19.8 percent are in full-time employment [89]. Pakistanis and Bangladeshis receive the highest rates of child benefits and among the highest rates of disability benefits. According to IFS (2022), migrants from Pakistan and Bangladesh contribute less in lifetime taxes than they receive in benefits, even into the third generation [90].

And then there's the Afghan scandal, perhaps the most damning revelation yet, broken in July 2025. For nearly two years, the British public was kept in the dark about a covert government program to resettle thousands of Afghan nationals in the UK. It began after a catastrophic data breach at the Ministry of Defence exposed the personal details of Afghan allies, prompting an emergency evacuation.

But what followed was not just a rescue operation; it was a demographic pipeline. Over 4,500 Afghans were quietly flown in under the radar, with plans to bring in up to 150,000 more through "family reunification."

The cost? As much as £7 billion, hidden from the public, never debated in Parliament, and excluded from any visible budget.

The scandal was protected by a super injunction so extreme that even the existence of the case could not be reported (more on this later). The media were gagged. Civil servants silenced. All under the pretext of national security and avoiding "community tensions."

However, this was not a matter of national security; it was a matter of national deception.

Now, with hundreds of Afghans suing the government for negligence, the financial and political fallout is only beginning [91].

For context, the £7 billion cost of the UK's secret Afghan resettlement scheme is nearly equal to the entire cost of NASA's Commercial Crew Program from 2011 to today. That program rebuilt America's ability to send astronauts into space, restored independent human spaceflight, and opened the door to the stars.

We could have had that. Instead, we got secret flights and media gag orders.

We traded the cosmos for cover-ups.

And that's just one trade. The Labour government recently cut the winter fuel allowance, a lifeline for the elderly, to save £1.4 billion. That's a choice that will kill British pensioners in their own homes.

The Afghan scheme costs nearly five times as much.

One decision leaves British pensioners to freeze. The other hands out homes and benefits to foreign arrivals. A country that sacrifices its old to fund its own demographic replacement isn't just in decline. It's been captured.

And that's just the financial cost. In the next chapter, we'll examine the social costs, the crime, the cultural tensions, and the brutal reality of importing this cohort of people at scale.

In Denmark, non-Western migrants and their descendants cost the state over €4 billion annually [92]. In Sweden, migration costs are estimated at €10 billion a year [93]. More than half of long-term welfare recipients are foreign-born. A 2020 government report found that second-generation non-European immigrants struggled with school completion and employment, suggesting integration worsens over time [94].

In the Netherlands, migrants from non-Western backgrounds cost taxpayers between €250,000 and €400,000 each over a lifetime [95]. Employment remains below 50 percent even after a decade has passed.

In the U.S., the Heritage Foundation estimated that each illegal immigrant household imposes a net burden of over $70,000. Sixty-three percent of non-citizen households use at least one welfare program [96]. California alone spends $30 billion annually on services for illegal immigrants [97]. Recently, the *Chicago Tribune* wrote a piece about immigrants "without legal status" losing their health care so Illinois could save $404 million. Until three seconds ago, we were told illegal immigrants didn't have access to social services like health care. Turns out they do, and it's been costing Americans billions.

In France, over half of non-European migrants are unemployed [98]. Fewer than one in three 2023 arrivals had a job by early 2024 [99]. In some regions, migrant unemployment rates exceed 50 percent. Migrants receive up to 2.6 times more in benefits than natives. Migrants are 15 times more likely to have tuberculosis and 40 times more likely to carry hepatitis B. A quarter of asylum seekers cite health as the reason for their migration into France [100].

In Canada, the federal government has spent $1.1 billion housing asylum seekers in hotels since 2017 [101]. Additionally, it has allocated another $1.5 billion to provinces and cities to help cover their expenses — including food, shelter, healthcare, legal aid, transit, and school placements. All of it paid for by the taxpayer. All of it prioritised.

That's $2.6 billion diverted not to struggling Canadians, not to homeless veterans, not to underfunded hospitals or collapsing infrastructure, but to foreign nationals who arrived without invitation, often without identification, and with no means of self-support.

While Canadian families face unaffordable rents and ballooning taxes, while people sleep in cars and line up at food banks, tens of thousands of asylum seekers are booked into hotels with hot meals, Wi Fi, and private bathrooms — some for months, some for years.

This isn't sustainable. It's national subsidisation of dysfunction.

The impact isn't limited to benefits. It affects wages. A National Bureau of Economic Research paper confirmed that low-skilled immigration depresses native wages, particularly for non-college-educated workers [102]. Migrant-heavy industries, such as construction and transportation, have seen stagnation or outright decline in real earnings.

Public infrastructure collapses under the strain. NHS doctors can't take new patients. The system spends hundreds of millions on translation services. Schools in high-immigration areas are often overcrowded and underperforming. Housing benefits and waitlists explode. Services once taken for granted buckle under the weight of imported demand.

We're told that mass migration is needed to fix our aging populations. However, even the UN acknowledges that to offset aging through immigration alone, Europe would require hundreds of millions of new arrivals.

You become what you import. You can't bring in millions of people from low-productivity, low-trust societies and expect those problems to vanish at the border. They persist in habits, expectations, and norms. Garrett Jones, in *The Culture Transplant*, makes this case clearly: migration transfers not just people, but values. Those values shape economies, politics, and institutions, sometimes for centuries.

Even generations later, descendants of immigrants continue to reflect their ancestral cultures in key economic attitudes. If you import people from societies that depend on state handouts and distrust individual responsibility, that shows up in policy, in elections, in budgets.

You don't just get new workers. You get new voters. And eventually, new outcomes.

This isn't just a policy mistake. It's a civilisational gamble.

And as technology advances, the gamble becomes even riskier. Because we're not just importing wage suppression. We're importing people into economies that will soon have no jobs for anyone. AI is rapidly consuming low-skilled work, including roles in retail, administration, call centres, and even parts of the transportation sector. Basic entry-level jobs are vanishing, replaced by machines and algorithms. Self-checkout kiosks. Automated warehouses. AI-powered help desks. It's not science fiction. It's now.

In this context, mass migration doesn't boost productivity. It swells dependency. It adds more mouths to feed while the pool of stable jobs shrinks. The result is an inverted pyramid: a narrow productive class, a bloated state apparatus, and a growing underclass.

Still, the open borders lobby pivots. When the economic argument collapses, they reach for a moral one: "It's not about economics — it's about values." They tell us diversity is our strength. That importing more differences will somehow bring more unity.

But what values, exactly? Diversity isn't a strength when it breaks solidarity. When the only thing people share is the queue at A&E. When trust frays, cohesion disappears, and resentment grows.

Think of what that money could fund. Schools. Cures. Exploration. Opportunity.

Instead, we fund translators. Welfare offices. Emergency housing.

We're not investing in our children. We're burning the inheritance.

This isn't just bad economics. It's a civilisational detour. A spacefaring society, shackled to tribal dysfunction. Billions spent managing decline while the future slips away.

But decline doesn't just drain your wallet. In the end, it comes for your safety too. Because when solidarity breaks, danger follows. And the price isn't just higher taxes, it's lives.

9

Rising Crime and Falling Safety

Mass migration has not just altered the look and feel of our cities. It has altered their safety, their culture, and their social fabric. We were promised "enrichment." What followed was a wave of low-level crime, scams, petty theft, businesses raided, and worse: murders, rapes, acid attacks, stabbings, and terror plots.

Mass migration from low-trust, tribal cultures does not just bring diversity. It brings danger. In places where the rule of law is weak, where women are not respected, and loyalty to tribe outweighs loyalty to nation, crime follows.

Harvard economist Eugen Dimant put it plainly: *"Immigration from corruption-ridden origin countries boosts corruption in the destination country."* In his 2019 paper, *"On Peer Effects: Behavioral Contagion of (Un)ethical Behavior and the Role of Social Identity,"* Dimant examines how individuals internalise behavioural norms from their country of origin, particularly regarding ethical conduct, and how these norms can influence their behaviour in new environments. The basic finding is sobering: corruption is contagious. People carry learned norms with them, and in the absence of strong institutional guardrails, those norms not only persist but also spread. Over time, this diffusion can begin to erode the institutional integrity of the host society. The result is not simply more bribery or rule-breaking; it is a slow normalisation of dysfunction [103].

Every Western government knows exactly which countries are broken. It literally publishes lists of places too dangerous for citizens to visit, such as Afghanistan, Syria, Yemen, Somalia, and South Sudan. Then it imports people from them. And we act surprised when dysfunction follows? Seriously, what did we think would happen?

In the 80s, the idea of a Canadian defecating on a public beach would have been unthinkable. Today, it has become disturbingly common. Cultural norms shift with cultural change. Bring in communities with regressive views on women, and you will see more harassment and assault. Bring in those who believe non-believers are fair game, and you will see more rape justified by ideology. Bring in those who see state systems as something to exploit, and you will see more scams, more benefit fraud, more illegal fishing, more fly tipping. Can you imagine a native Brit eating a swan? Of course not. But now, swans are being eaten in the UK.

You have probably heard some version of this excuse: "But English people commit crimes too." Yes, we have our criminals. But migrants are statistically overrepresented in crime across every category. And just because we have homegrown rapists does not mean we should import more.

Recall from the last chapter, where we discussed the 150,000 Afghans being brought to the UK? If you are wondering how assimilation has gone for Afghans elsewhere in Europe, the data is sobering. In Germany, they commit gang rape at over 40 times the rate of ethnic Germans. Even Afghan women alone are 26 percent more likely to be suspects in violent crime than German males [104].

How could we have guessed this would happen? Well, perhaps a culture known for practicing bacha bāzī, where boys are dressed as girls, forced to dance, and raped by grown men, was not going to make the West safer.

These are not isolated incidents. They reflect deeply rooted norms and values. When we open the door to mass migration without demanding alignment on basic moral standards, we do not just get diversity, we get danger. Real people. Real victims. Abused and killed because our leaders were too cowardly to draw a line.

An Afghan man arrives in Britain illegally. He tells authorities he is 14 years old. He is not; he is closer to 20. He is placed in a school with children. Given housing. Fed. Protected. No one checks his background. No one dares. His name is Lawangeen Abdulrahimzai, and before setting foot in the UK, he had already murdered two men in Serbia. He was not hiding it. Serbian authorities had issued a warrant for his arrest. But Britain did not bother to look. Instead, the system gave him sanctuary and a new start. He repaid that trust by stabbing 21-year-old Thomas Roberts to death in the street. Thomas had tried to intervene in a petty argument outside a club in Bournemouth. He was due to start training with the Royal Marines. He wanted to serve his country. The country let him die. The killer was protected. Thomas was sacrificed [105].

Then there was Kasaj, an illegal migrant out on bail from a detention centre. He went on to kill two people and attempt to murder a third, random strangers on the street, while still in the country unlawfully. And Koci Selamaj, an Albanian migrant, who walked up behind 28-year-old teacher Sabina Nessa as she crossed a London park, and beat her to death with a metal traffic sign. No connection. No warning. Just another woman targeted and murdered by a man who should never have been here.

In Germany, Maria Ladenburger is cycling home from a party in Freiburg. She is 19. A medical student. Her father is a senior lawyer with the European Commission. Her family supports refugee resettlement and opens their home to help new arrivals integrate into the community. One of those arrivals is Hussein Khavari, another Afghan migrant who told authorities he was 17. He was not. He had already been convicted of attempted murder in Greece, he threw a woman off a cliff during a robbery, and was released early. After that, he slipped into Germany, lied again, and was welcomed once more. That night, he raped Maria and dumped her body in a river. Her family believed in the system. The system welcomed her killer [106].

Then there is Mia Valentin. Just 15 years old. She had been dating a migrant boy, another Afghan who claimed to be underage and was placed in school. The relationship soured. Mia tried to break up with him. He did not take it well. One day, he followed her into a drugstore and stabbed her to death in front of horrified staff and customers. The state had labelled him a "child refugee." He was not. He was a grown man with a knife. Mia thought he was a classmate. He was a predator in disguise [107].

And in France, the tragedy took a national dimension. Samuel Paty was a secondary school teacher in a suburb of Paris. He believed in liberal values, free thought, open debate, and freedom of speech. During a civics lesson, he showed the class the Charlie Hebdo cartoons of Muhammad. He warned students beforehand and gave them the option to leave. He believed that education required courage. A Chechen refugee named Abdullakh Anzorov, radicalised online, disagreed. Days later, he waited outside the school, tracked Paty down, and beheaded him in the street with a kitchen knife. France had given Anzorov asylum. Had fed him, housed him, schooled him. In return, he turned a quiet suburb into a scene of Islamist horror. France gave him shelter. He gave France a corpse [108].

These are not isolated stories. They are the inevitable consequences of a system that refuses to ask questions, refuses to protect its own, and punishes suspicion more harshly than it punishes violence. Each of these victims had a future. Each was killed by someone who never should have been there.

We have seen it all too often now: a quiet town, a few hundred to a few thousand people, the kind of place where doors go unlocked and everyone knows the butcher's dog. Then, one day, the buses arrive. No vote. No warning. Just a sudden notice, if that. A former hotel or office building is converted into an asylum centre, where migrants are housed indefinitely. Locals are told to be welcoming. To show compassion.

Then the stories begin. A girl followed home from school. A woman harassed outside a shop. Shoplifting. Fights. A stabbing near the pub. It is not every migrant, but it is enough. Enough to change how people walk at night. Enough to make mothers nervous. The town holds a meeting. Locals show up angry, scared, and confused. They ask who approved this, who is accountable, and whom they can speak to. No one gives a straight answer. The councillors dodge. The police speak in circles. The media does not show up, not yet. So the locals take it into their own hands. They organise. They hold signs. They protest outside the centre. Some wear masks, afraid of being doxxed. They demand answers. But the government ignores them. The NGOs double down. Tensions rise.

And then someone throws paint. Or breaks a window. Or, as happened in Ireland recently, builds a migrant effigy and sets it alight, a symbolic act of fury after yet another brutal attack. That is when the media finally arrives. But not to ask why people are angry, or to investigate the crimes that sparked the outrage. They come to condemn the reaction. Far right violence. Racist mobs. Dangerous misinformation.

The original story, the harassment, the fear, and the broken trust disappear. Now the threat is not the crime. It is the locals. Police arrive not to protect them, but to film faces, collect names, and open files. The state will not ask what drove them to protest. It will ensure they never do it again.

And so the cycle repeats. Town after town. Country after country. A migrant commits a crime. A community reacts. The media attacks the community. The government covers its ears. Nothing changes.

These people should not have to march, or shout, or burn anything. They should not have to gamble their jobs or reputations just to say the simplest truth: we do not feel safe anymore.

If the state did its job, if it protected its people and preserved their way of life, none of this would be necessary.

But it doesn't, so it is.

"When society is orderly, you protect yourself with justice. When society is chaotic, you protect justice by yourself."

— The Huainanzi (139 B.C.)

And notice, these illegal migrant hotels and asylum centers are never placed in the Cotswolds. Not in Surrey. Not in Mayfair, Chelsea, Westminster, Pimlico, Fitzrovia, or Chiswick. Everywhere the elite live and play remains untouched. They know exactly what it would do to their community if they did. So it's only *your* community that's sacrificed.

When you import people from lawless cultures, without documentation, without vetting, and without limits, you do not just get refugees. You get rapists, killers, and jihadists, too. And when it happens, as it always does, our leaders look shocked. They light candles. They say, "This is not who we are." But they never say, "This is who he was. And this is why he never should have been let in."

When you dig into the statistics across the West, they tell a bleak story. In Germany, crime rose 5.5% in 2023 [109]. The number of identified suspects increased by 7.3%, indicating a broader rise in criminal investigations and arrests [109]. Foreigners accounted for 41% of all suspects, representing a 17.8% increase [109]. Asylum seekers, just 2.5% of the population, accounted for 18% of all offenders and 13.1% of sexual assault suspects [109]. Knife crime has tripled since 2020. Violent crime is at a 15-year high. Even female immigrants from countries like Syria, Afghanistan, Bulgaria, Iraq, and Serbia commit violent crimes at higher rates than native German men.

In North Rhine-Westphalia:

- 80% of pickpockets were foreign nationals [110]
- 47% of shoplifters and burglars [110]
- 41.6% of homicide suspects [110]
- 37.1% of violent sex crime suspects [110]

Germany's 2015 New Year's Eve attacks in Cologne saw over 1,200 women sexually assaulted by mobs of migrant background men [111]. Even top politicians are now speaking out. CDU's Herbert Reul said bluntly, "We have a problem with non-German criminals." What was once dismissed as far-right scaremongering is now being echoed by the establishment.

A 2005 Swedish government report found foreign-born men were five times more likely to be suspected of rape than native Swedes

[112]. Reported sexual offences rose 44% between 2006 and 2018 [113]. A 2017 SVT investigation found 58% of men convicted of rape were foreign-born [114]. And then by 2025, a peer-reviewed study from Lund University examined convictions for rape (including aggravated and attempted) in Sweden between 2000 and 2020. It found that about 63% of those convicted had a first or second-generation immigrant background. It is getting worse, not better.

In Austria, migrants are responsible for over 55% of sexual assaults in Vienna, despite being under 20% of the population [115].

In Norway, a 2011 Oslo police report found that 100% of aggravated stranger rapes over five years were committed by non-Western immigrants, mostly from Muslim majority countries [116].

In Finland, foreigners commit 43% of all rapes, while making up only 8% of the population [117].

In Switzerland, Eritrean asylum seekers were 35 times more likely to commit serious violent crimes than native Swiss [118].

The same trend is unfolding across the Atlantic. In the US, mass migration has fuelled welfare fraud, gang violence, human trafficking, and rising violent crime. The Center for Immigration Studies reports illegal immigrants are arrested for violent crimes at higher rates than native born citizens in several states. The Texas Department of Public Safety states that most arrests near the border now involve illegal migrants. Cities with large undocumented populations have seen surges in gang activity, drug trafficking, and systemic exploitation of public services. Influxes of Haitian migrants have overwhelmed border cities and states, with spikes in drug crime, violent assaults, and property offences.

In Minneapolis, once known for its Scandinavian civility and progressive calm, Somali immigrant communities have been involved in a massive autism welfare fraud scheme. Thousands of families submitted fake diagnoses to siphon government funds, costing taxpayers millions and denying care to those who genuinely need it.

In 2012, federal prosecutors dismantled a massive Somali-run sex trafficking ring operating out of Minneapolis. The victims were young, some just twelve years old. They were groomed, abused, and transported across state lines for prostitution. The gang even branded some of the girls with tattoos to mark ownership. It was not a lone predator. It was an organised network. A cultural import. And the justice system took notice, convictions followed, but the story barely made national headlines.

A decade later came something even bigger. During the COVID-19 pandemic, Minnesota became the site of one of the largest fraud cases in U.S. history. More than $250 million in federal relief funds, meant to feed low-income children, were siphoned off by a criminal conspiracy primarily involving Somali immigrants. The scheme exploited emergency food programs by fabricating rosters of children and billing the government for meals that were never served. Dozens have been charged. Mansions, luxury cars, and overseas wire transfers tell the rest of the story. And while legal proceedings are ongoing, the scale of the alleged theft is staggering.

In London, knife crime is now the leading cause of death for teenage boys. The majority of suspects are black or South Asian, largely from migrant backgrounds. This is not random violence. It is the direct result of imported tribalism, postcode wars, and ethnic gang structures. It used to be youthful mischief. Now it is urban warfare.

The UK Government, under FOI requests, released crime data by ethnicity [119]:

- **Algerians**: 18 times more likely to be convicted of theft
- **Congolese**: 12 times more likely for violent crime

- **Somalians**: 8 times more likely
- **Afghans and Eritreans**: 20 times more likely to be convicted of sexual offences
- **Foreign nationals overall**: 71% more likely to be convicted of sex crimes

Every eight minutes, a phone is stolen in London. I do not know a single Londoner who has not experienced it. Friends chased mopeds through traffic. Colleagues robbed at café tables. One friend had her phone snatched mid-call on Oxford Street, in the middle of the day, with crowds everywhere. Police told her to file an online report. That was it. No follow-up. No interest.

And if you go online, you will see the truth that no one will say out loud. Countless videos of migrants robbing, harassing, and stalking people on the tube. Packs of men surrounding lone women. Hands in pockets. Phones snatched. Bags torn away. Not just once. Every day. And what did we think would happen?

And the effect is palpable. A recent UK poll found that 57 percent of women no longer feel safe walking alone in London [120]. Nearly half say they have been followed. These are not abstract fears; they are daily realities. The streets are not what they used to be, no matter what London Mayor Sadiq Khan claims. The city's leadership insists that things are improving, but the people living there know better. They sense the change in their routines, in their instincts, and in the way they navigate public space. Safety has become a privilege, not a baseline.

This is the direct result of policies that prioritise optics over safety, diversity over truth, and image over protection. European women are living the consequences of mass migration, not in theory, but in their daily lives. From rising harassment in public spaces to the quiet erosion of hard-won freedoms, the cultural clash unfolding around them is no longer a matter of denial. What was once dismissed as far-right scaremongering is now being spoken aloud, first in whispers, then in organised movements, such as the Women's Safety Initiative.

These women are not driven by ideology but by instinct and evidence, by the recognition that the society around them is no longer safe, and that no one in power will admit why. It is fast becoming socially acceptable for women to oppose mass immigration, and it is triggering a preference cascade; millions are realising they are not alone, and they are speaking out.

This collapse of safety is most apparent in the UK Grooming Gang scandal. For decades, perhaps as early as the 70s, hundreds of thousands of native British girls, overwhelmingly white, working class, and vulnerable, were systematically raped, drugged, and trafficked by networks of predominantly Pakistani Muslim men.

In Rotherham alone, at least 1,400 girls were exploited between 1997 and 2013. The same pattern repeated in Rochdale, Oxford, Telford, Huddersfield, and beyond. Authorities — police, social workers, council officials — knew. And did nothing. Not out of ignorance, but out of fear: fear of being called racist, of offending community leaders, of losing their jobs. Some councillors were complicit. Political correctness was placed above child protection.

A 2020 Home Office report finally confirmed what the public already knew: most of the convicted men were of Pakistani heritage, and the victims were almost entirely white British girls (Sikhs were also targeted) [121]. Whistleblowers estimate the actual number of victims could exceed 250,000 over the past thirty years [122].

A quarter of a million British girls. Raped. Drugged. Pimped out. And for years, ignored.

The media tried to downplay it. Politicians looked the other way. But the truth broke through. Elon Musk, not a British leader, helped push the issue back into public view using his global platform. That is how broken the system is: it took a billionaire outsider to say what no one in power dared to.

And what is Britain doing now? Police are running PowerPoint presentations in asylum hotels, through translators, explaining to new arrivals that it is not acceptable to harass schoolgirls, loiter outside primary schools, or film women in public. That is how far we have fallen. The basics, do not follow children, do not touch them, do not rape them, now have to be taught like fire safety.

This was not just a scandal. It was a collapse of culture. And it is still ongoing.

This is not a condemnation of all migrants. It is a demand for decency. If we cannot protect the vulnerable in our own communities, what moral authority do we have left?

Terrorism did not sneak in. It walked in. For years, we were told that open borders and cultural sensitivity were moral progress. But they also opened us up to a different kind of threat, one that does not just steal wallets, but lives.

In 2005, coordinated suicide bombings in London killed 52 people and injured 700. The attackers were British-born Muslims, three of Pakistani descent. Raised under British laws. Schooled in British systems. And still, they grew to hate the country that gave them everything [123].

The same pattern repeated. In 2017, a bomb exploded at a children's concert in Manchester Arena. Twenty-two people were killed, many of them teenage girls. The attacker, Salman Abedi, was the son of Libyan migrants granted asylum in Britain. He repaid that kindness with blood [124].

London Bridge. Westminster. Streatham. Reading. The names and bodies pile up. And yet, the justifications keep coming.

In France, the jihadist crisis is even more severe. Charlie Hebdo. The Bataclan. The Nice truck attack. These were not just attacks; they were declarations of war. That free speech, music, joy itself, are punishable by death.

These killers did not come from the outside. They came from within. From no-go zones like Seine-Saint-Denis and Molenbeek. Urban enclaves where French law no longer applies. Where jihadist ideology is preached openly. Where the state has ceded authority to gangs, radical clerics, and foreign-funded mosques.

Weapons are hidden in prayer halls. Martyrs are made in prison cells. Muslims make up 12% of France's population but 70% of its prison population [125]. And those prisons do not rehabilitate. They radicalise.

A cell of women once plotted to bomb Notre Dame. A Tunisian man drove a truck through a Bastille Day crowd, killing 84. His accomplice returned to film the bodies. This is not extremism on the margins. It is an ecosystem.

In the US, the 2015 San Bernardino attack saw a married couple murder 14 people at a Christmas party. Syed Farook was U.S.-born, the son of Pakistani immigrants. His wife, Tashfeen Malik, was a Pakistani national who had passed background checks and entered the country on a legal visa. They pledged allegiance to ISIS [126].

They did not sneak in. They were welcomed.

This is not a failure to integrate. It is a refusal to assimilate. Political Islam is not just a private faith. It is a political system that does not want to coexist; it wants to dominate. It demands submission from non-believers, whether through conversion, subjugation, or war. This is not fringe. It is mainstream doctrine in much of the Islamic world. And when you import it en masse, you do not get diversity. You get a collision. Parallel societies. And eventually, blood.

In July 2024, Axel Rudakubana, a 17-year-old of Rwandan heritage, stabbed 14 children in a Southport dance class. Three girls, aged six, seven, and nine, were killed. He had stockpiled ricin, owned an al Qaeda manual, and had been referred to Prevent three times. Nothing was done. In 2025, he was sentenced to life with a minimum of 52 years [127].

During the trial, he expressed delight that children had died. The media portrayed him as a typical Welsh boy because he was born in Wales. Is Axel Rudakubana as Welsh as Tom Jones? Only a feckless idiot would say yes. Let's call a spade a spade: he is a migrant, with a Welsh passport, filled with rage and Islamist ideological rot. If his parents had not been allowed into the country, those little girls would be alive.

But fine, let's play along. Let's say he was Welsh, just like the media insists. Doesn't that make it even worse? Doesn't that prove assimilation is not working? If a boy raised on British soil still grows up to hate the country and its people, what exactly are we assimilating into?

The truth is, a passport does not make you British any more than owning a stethoscope makes you a surgeon. They play this trick all the time. Someone commits a sexual crime. Media reports that a "Yorkshireman" was the perpetrator. A quick Google search reveals the name: Zainal Osman. Ah, yes, as Yorkshire as the Brontë sisters.

Every crime report now sounds like a Monty Python sketch: 'A Burnley man named Muhammad Ali.' They think we are idiots.

None of this is accidental. You do not build spin propaganda like this to protect people; you build it to protect an agenda. Because the truth is fragile. The promises of harmony, enrichment, and seamless integration have not been delivered. And so, instead of confronting reality, the system targets those who speak it. And increasingly, it punishes speech more harshly than actual crime.

This is why the state has built an entire censorship apparatus, not to prevent harm, but to prevent disruption of the story. In 2023, a brutal crime was committed in Britain. A young girl was assaulted by an Afghan migrant, a case so severe it would have made national headlines, sparked public outrage, and reopened debates around asylum policy. But the story never reached the public. Instead, a super injunction was issued. Not only was the attacker's identity hidden, but the existence of the case itself was concealed. The media was gagged. Court proceedings were locked behind closed doors. Official silence descended. The British public was not allowed to know, not just who did it, but that it even happened at all [128].

This was not an isolated failure of the justice system. It was an intentional suppression of truth. The rationale? To avoid "stoking community tensions." In other words, the safety and rights of British children were deemed less necessary than the reputational image of imported communities. The system chose optics over justice.

When the state hides migrant crime from its own citizens, it is no longer acting in their interest. It is managing them. Gaslighting them. The Afghan super injunction was not an effort to guarantee a fair trial; it was a desperate attempt to protect a narrative. A narrative of multicultural harmony, of moral progress, of benevolent resettlement. One that cannot survive exposure to reality.

This is the same impulse behind the manipulation of crime data, the redaction of offender demographics, the quiet renaming of "grooming gangs" to "urban exploitation networks." It is all part of the same machinery: obscure the truth, criminalise the dissent, and cast anyone who notices as a bigot. What we are witnessing is not transparency or accountability. It is rule by euphemism and omission. A government more afraid of offending imported sensibilities than defending its own people.

Across Europe, new laws claim to fight "hate speech" and "disinformation," while governments lean on tech platforms to silence dissent. The EU, with Britain on a leash despite what Brexit was meant to deliver, has morphed into the USSR—sclerotic, corrupt, obsessed with censorship, fiercely anti-democratic, complete with an unelected nomenklatura led by the likes of Ursula von der Leyen. Bankrupt ideologically and soon literally, it is unloved, unfeared, and unfixable.

Britain isn't just going along with this drift; it's leading it. Under policies like "non-crime hate incidents," you can be investigated, logged, and flagged for saying something politically incorrect—even if you've broken no law. These reports can sit on your record, appear in background checks, and you may never even know they exist.

Police won't lift a finger if your phone's stolen or your car's broken into. They'll shrug, file a report, and send you on your way. But call someone the wrong word online? Expect a platoon of police at your door the next day. Britain: soft on crime, hard on opinions.

Meanwhile, groups like Hope Not Hate and Tell MAMA are funded by the government to monitor speech and label "extremism"—a term now stretched to include ordinary citizens expressing valid concerns about immigration, culture, or crime.

The UK's new Online Safety Act hands sweeping power to the state to decide what counts as "legal but harmful," effectively criminalising moral discomfort. It was sold as a way to protect children from harmful content. Instead, it was almost immediately used to suppress coverage of protests at migrant hotels. A law meant for child-protection has become a tool of censorship—shutting down reporting and debate the public has a right to see.

It's the perfect snapshot of a country upside down. Bureaucracy clamps down on ordinary people for the smallest, pettiest things — ID checks for a website, forms for cough syrup, warnings for words. Yet for those breaking in by boat, there are no forms, no checks, no questions. The rules tighten for the citizen while they dissolve for the outsider. You now need a passport to watch porn — but not to enter the UK on a boat.

All this censoriousness is designed to protect the illusion. The illusion of harmony. The illusion that mass migration is working. And above all, the illusion that dissent is dangerous. As of July 2025, they've even assembled a specialized "elite" police unit to scour social media for "anti-migrant sentiment," tasked with flagging "early signs of potential civil unrest."

The British State is pursuing its policy not of changing the thing that the people object to, but punishing the people who notice the thing, instead. In a way, it's a backhanded positive sign. They're desperate. As George Orwell said, *"All tyrannies rule through fraud and force, but once the fraud is exposed, they must rely exclusively on force."*

They're losing. It's the deep state's panic button, a last-ditch attempt to choke off dissent by dressing up censorship as "protection" and trying to suppress visible signs of dissent, a battle they will not win. It's a playbook, and people see through it. Fear isn't working anymore.

Another glaring example of hypocrisy: in June 2025, two foreign delivery drivers were convicted of sexually assaulting a 14-year-old girl in her home. They were sentenced to two and a half years [129]. Contrast that with the case of Lucy Connolly, a British mother, who posted a politically incorrect tweet about migrants after the massacre of three young girls in Southport. She deleted it. No violence. No victims. She got two years and seven months [130]—more time for a tweet than for raping a child.

The same is happening all across the West. Take Canada. Trucker protest organisers like Tamara Lich and Chris Barber face years in prison for non-violent dissent, while immigrant offenders guilty of far worse often walk free. Google Manpreet Gill, Akashkumar Khant, and Samarpreet Singh, and read the details of each case. One helped cause a crash that killed four (including a baby). One tried to buy sex from a minor. One person exposed himself inside a woman's home. All received very light sentences. In each case, judges cited immigration status or citizenship concerns as reasons for leniency. Protest the state, and you are punished. Commit serious crimes, and you are protected.

This is not justice. It is a hierarchy, one where speech is punished more severely than violence, so long as the violence comes from someone the state fears to confront. If you commit a horrific crime and tick the right demographic boxes, you get leniency. But if you speak an uncomfortable truth, you get crushed.

You are met with shame, not for what you have said, but for who you are. Told to sit down, stay quiet, and carry the weight of things done long before you were born. Your past disqualifies your future. Your heritage cancels your voice.

It is not enough to accept the changes. You are expected to repent for them. Because in this story, decline is not a tragedy; it is justice. And that is the next lie we need to face.

10

The Sins of the Father

One of the most toxic justifications for mass migration is the idea of inherited guilt.

"You colonised us, now we're here to take over."
"Europe exploited the world; the world gets to move in."
"This is payback."

This is not immigration policy. It is tribal revenge, repackaged as virtue. Not migration, but reverse colonialism. Only this time, the invaders come armed not with muskets, but with moral leverage. "You owe us," they say. And we hand them the keys.

This "immigration is revenge" argument is always revealing, because it acknowledges — without intending to — that these immigrants are actually a blight on the societies they grace with their presence.

For the modern left, mass immigration into the West is not just a policy. It is ideology. It is about reshaping the demographic makeup of historically Western nations as a form of revenge or "justice," and redistributing wealth from those who built these societies to those who didn't. It is not compassion. It is retribution disguised as progress.

I do not believe the consequences of mass migration are just the result of government failure. When something continues despite its clear and mounting costs, you have to ask whether it is a malfunction or a design. I think the goal of mass migration, and the multiculturalism that trails behind it, was never to improve the lives of citizens, but to break apart the shared culture, religion, and national story that once gave Western nations meaning. The result? No-go zones in Paris. Grooming gangs in Britain. Firebombs in Sweden. All symptoms of deeper fractures are justified as revenge for the supposed ravages of colonialism. And that fracture creates the perfect conditions for a population that is easier to manage, distract, and control.

Yes, European powers once held empires. So did everyone else. The Ottomans, Arabs, Mongols, Zulus, Chinese, Aztecs, and Japanese all built empires through conquest, slavery, and domination. Empire is not uniquely European. It is the story of civilisation.

But no one tells Japan to open its borders because of Manchuria. No one demands Morocco take in a million Spaniards for centuries of piracy and slavery. No one insists that Turkey repay the Balkans for the Ottoman yoke.

I am tired of the language of "decolonising." If we are serious about dismantling the legacies of empire, let us not stop with the West. The Ottomans ruled the Balkans. The Mughals ruled India. The Umayyads and Abbasids spread through North Africa and Spain. All Islamic. So, when do we decolonise Turkey, Pakistan, Morocco, or the Middle East? Or is "decolonisation" just a selective tool, designed not to challenge empire, but to humiliate the West?

Only the West moralises itself into erasure. Why? Because Western civilisation internalised guilt. Christianity gave us sin, shame, and redemption. The Enlightenment layered on abstraction: universal rights, equality, progress. These worked when the West had confidence. Now, they have become weapons turned inward. "Love thy neighbour" became "import the world." Mass migration is not framed as policy. It is framed as penance.

Suicidal empathy, as Gad Saad describes it, is the self-destructive impulse to prioritise the feelings of others — even hostile outsiders — over the survival of your own culture. It is what happens when pathological altruism overtakes reason, when compassion is weaponised against those who possess it. The West, in its desperate bid to be seen as tolerant and virtuous, welcomes the intolerant, excuses the inexcusable, and sacrifices its future on the altar of moral posturing. This is not kindness. It is cowardice. As Saad warns, a society that elevates feelings over facts, inclusion over identity, and guilt over self-preservation is one that has chosen extinction with a smile.

All empires committed atrocities, then moved on and built myths of glory. Their descendants high-five their ancestors. Ours tear down their statues. This is not universal morality; it is cultural masochism. No one lectures Mongolia about its genocides. No one tells Nigeria to reflect on its centuries of internal slavery. No one demands Morocco open its borders. Western guilt is selective. Performative. And uniquely self-destructive.

Countries like England, France, Germany, and Sweden are told that their only moral option is to dissolve. That if their ancestors did bad things, their descendants must pay the price, forever. But I do not owe someone a house, healthcare, and free school meals because my great-great-granduncle exported tea from Bengal. That is not justice; it is vengeance. And it is being weaponised against the very societies that once stood for liberalism, openness, and the rule of law.

Let us set aside, for a moment, the fact that the British were arguably the least terrible empire in history. They built infrastructure. They introduced administrative systems. They believed, even if imperfectly, that they had obligations to those they ruled. The point is not that colonialism was good — the point is that inherited guilt is not a moral framework. It is a rejection of one.

Inherited guilt undermines the foundation of the West: the idea that individuals are judged by their actions, not their ancestry. That rights are personal, not collective. That you do not punish someone for being born on the "wrong" side of history. We do not give out prison sentences to grandchildren. We do not demolish homes because someone's ancestor committed a crime in 1850. We did not build Western civilisation on shame. At least, we didn't. And yet, that is what is happening now.

Yes, the U.S. and the West more broadly have a long history of foreign policy failure. Regime changes, proxy wars, and interventions in the Middle East have destabilised entire regions. But that does not mean we import the instability we created. Bombing Libya does not mean Minneapolis should absorb Somali clan networks and see its welfare systems exploited. Toppling Saddam does not mean a small Texas town should be flooded with undocumented migrants and watch its schools, hospitals, and police services collapse.

Why should an American nurse, truck driver, or teacher bear the cost of political decisions they never supported? The people responsible for these failures, politicians, diplomats, NGOs, live in gated communities. They do not sit in ERs for hours. Their daughters are not followed home. They do not have to explain to their kids why their schools no longer function. It is always ordinary citizens who pay the price.

Mass migration is no longer framed as a way to build a better future. It is framed as punishment for past sins. And that creates a dangerous dynamic: importing millions of people who do not see themselves as joining, but as settling scores. If resentment is the reason for coming, why are we letting them in? This is not immigration. It is demographic warfare. Not with tanks and guns, but with birthrates, ballots, and benefits. Not a war for land, but for legacy.

You cannot import people who believe your country is evil and expect harmony. You cannot shame a population into erasing itself and expect gratitude in return. And we are already seeing the consequences. Schools rewriting history to portray the West as uniquely malevolent. Political parties focused on identity blocs rather than shared national interests. Cities fractured into parallel societies instead of cohesive communities. Even terror attacks are now reframed as justified "blowback" for colonialism, as if murder is just another invoice from history.

Mass migration is not a sacred obligation. It is a political choice. And we are allowed to say no. Because your children were not born to balance history's books. They were born to inherit a home and to keep it whole.

But shame has an expiry date. Eventually, even guilt-fatigued nations reach for a softer lie, one that promises peace without sacrifice: They will assimilate.

But even if the shame fades, the damage doesn't. Because guilt didn't just change who we welcomed, it changed who we are.

11

Assimilate to What?

We often ask why immigrants don't assimilate. Why don't they adopt our customs, our language, our laws, our values? But rarely do we stop to ask a more uncomfortable question: assimilate into what?

It's not entirely the fault of migrants that they don't conform. Because conformity implies a standard. A shape. A shared sense of who we are. And that's precisely what we've lost.

In the United States, how do you assimilate into a nation that can't decide whether it was founded in liberty or in sin? Where 1776 competes with 1619. Where schoolchildren are taught that the Founding Fathers were genocidal slavers and the Constitution a relic of white supremacy. Where the national anthem is booed at sports games and the flag is seen as a symbol of oppression, while foreign banners are waved with pride. What exactly are migrants meant to be loyal to?

In Canada, assimilation is treated as offensive. The Prime Minister has openly declared the country a "post-national state" with "no core identity." This is not a bug, it's the design. Canada doesn't ask newcomers to become Canadian because it no longer knows what

Canadian means. Instead, it repackages guilt as virtue. The country defines itself not by culture or achievement, but by apology. To be Canadian is to apologise for existing on stolen land, to signal one's shame, to submit. How can anyone integrate into a nation that sees its own founding as a crime scene?

In England, the cradle of Magna Carta and Shakespeare, the rot runs just as deep. Statues of Churchill are boarded up like criminals. St George's Cross is treated like a hate symbol. British history is taught as a catalogue of sins, never of triumphs. Meanwhile, Islamist preachers shout freely in the streets. Foreign flags hang from government buildings. Entire boroughs operate under customs and norms imported wholesale.

And in our universities — the very institutions that once preserved and passed down Western civilisation — we now have students in keffiyehs and faculty chanting "Hey hey, ho ho, Western civ has got to go." These aren't rebels. They're heirs burning their own inheritance, too brainwashed or bitter to see what they're losing. They are dismantling the very thing worth assimilating into. You can't integrate into a void. You can't build loyalty on a foundation of shame. And you can't expect immigrants to love a country that doesn't love itself.

France tried harder. The state aggressively pushed laïcité — secular assimilation — through schools, laws, and civic culture. But when migrant communities rejected French norms, the state backed down. Today, there are over 750 no-go zones in France — zones urbaines sensibles — where French law is secondary to tribal loyalty. Riots erupt at any perceived insult to Islam. Teachers are beheaded in the street for defending free speech. The state offers platitudes. France wanted assimilation, but lacked the will to enforce it.

Sweden took a different path. It welcomed migrants with open arms and closed eyes. It preached tolerance and neutrality while importing people who reject both. Today, Sweden — once the safest country in the world — has some of Europe's highest rates of gun crime, grenade attacks, and clan-based violence. Parallel societies emerged almost overnight. Swedish feminists now march in hijabs to prove their tolerance to communities that do not reciprocate it. Sweden didn't ask migrants to assimilate. It begged not to offend them. That is the core of the crisis.

Assimilation is not magic. It requires clarity, conviction, and confidence. A society that knows who it is can extend a hand and say, "You are welcome here, but here, this is who we are."

But when that identity dissolves into self-hatred, when the national mythos is dismantled and replaced with shame, what are newcomers supposed to become? We cannot ask others to believe in something we're too cowardly to defend. We say we want integration, but we're terrified of asserting ourselves. We'd rather be called tolerant than be right. We'd rather celebrate their culture than preserve our own.

This is the fatal flaw of multiculturalism. It doesn't ask people to join. It tells them to remain as they are. It doesn't build one culture; it entrenches many, in parallel, even when they clash. "Multi" doesn't mean unity. It means silos. Separate laws. Separate customs. Separate allegiances. That's not integration. It's fragmentation.

We used to believe in assimilation, the idea that newcomers should adapt to the host culture. That belief built nations. Multiculturalism dismantles them. And when you elevate "diversity" above coherence, you end up with a country that's no longer a nation. Just a map with borders.

Here lies the great paradox: immigration into the West exploded just as the West lost faith in itself. We opened the gates, then burned down the temple. We invited the world in, then forgot what home was.

So what's the result? Parallel societies. Ethnic enclaves. Clashing norms. Not because migrants are inherently unwilling to adapt, but because we no longer give them a destination. Because we've replaced civilisational confidence with cultural relativism.

If we want assimilation, we need to be something worth assimilating into. That means regaining pride. Not empty nationalism, but a real sense of who we are and what we stand for. It means teaching our children that they are heirs to something great. The civilisation of Plato and Da Vinci. Of Newton, Jefferson, and Shakespeare. The civilisation that birthed the cathedral and the symphony. The novel and the scientific method.

The West is not perfect. But it is exceptional. And if we don't say so, no one else will. We must reclaim our myths. Revive our stories. And speak once more with the voice of a people who know who they are.

Because if we don't, others will fill the vacuum. And what replaces us won't be kinder. Or freer. It will be louder, stronger, and utterly alien.

This isn't just a political or cultural breakdown. It's psychological. When identity collapses, so does meaning. And the people who were born here are often the ones who suffer most — quietly and alone.

12

The Soul Displaced

M ass immigration is often framed in economic or moral terms. Politicians speak of labour shortages, GDP growth, or humanitarian duty. Corporations praise diversity as a strength. But beneath these abstract ideals lies a quiet epidemic of psychological distress, an unease felt not by the newcomers, but by those who never moved an inch and now find themselves strangers in the places they once called home.

This is not a rejection of migrants as people. It's a reckoning with the emotional and existential toll imposed on native populations by rapid, large-scale demographic change. What happens when the world around you transforms faster than you can adapt? When the culture, symbols, language, and rituals you grew up with vanish in the span of a decade?

The modern mind treats identity like an accessory, something to be chosen, swapped, or discarded at will. But for most, identity is not optional. It is an inherited structure. It gives coherence to memory. It tells you where you belong, what your duties are, and how to navigate life. When that scaffold collapses, so does the psyche. Community dissolves into a crowd. Ritual becomes performance. Meaning thins. The result is confusion, anxiety, depression, and often, rage.

People feel psychologically displaced when their environment changes too fast. The language shifts. Local customs vanish. The songs and stories they knew as children disappear. They are told their discomfort is backward. That nostalgia is racism. But what they feel isn't hate, it's grief.

Displacement doesn't require a suitcase. For the native working class, it's dislocation without movement. The corner shop changes. The pub closes. The sounds on the street no longer feel familiar. They are told to celebrate this. That resistance is immoral. So a second wound is inflicted: not just alienation, but shame.

In Rotterdam, a Dutch schoolboy refused to chant the Islamic call to prayer during a "multicultural celebration." He wasn't hateful, just uncomfortable. He was reprimanded. Labelled intolerant. In the name of tolerance, his right to dissent was erased. This is the new contract: not coexistence, but submission.

In Birmingham's Sparkbrook, the last pub closed after a century. The new population didn't drink. The landlord received threats. No headlines marked its passing. But with every shuttered gathering place, a culture bleeds out. In parts of Luton and Bradford, councils stopped putting up Christmas lights. Officially, it was about budgets or "inclusivity." Residents noticed. But most said nothing.

In North West London, a scout group folded. Local parents objected to camping, to singing, to boys and girls mixing. In one Midlands town, only elderly veterans turned up at the cenotaph. The crowd around them didn't observe the silence. Not out of malice, but because the moment meant nothing to them.

At a state school with a growing conservative Muslim intake, sports day was first segregated, then cancelled altogether. In Manchester, a community centre that once hosted music classes now contains gender segregated prayer rooms. The piano still sits in the corner, untouched. Even newcomers feel it. An Afghan interpreter, promised safety in the UK, said his children are growing up "neither Afghan nor British." He didn't come to erase a culture. He came to join one. Now, there is nothing clear to join.

What happened to the East London cockneys, their quiet erasure from the tapestry of English life, is happening across the country. In the Medway towns, proud of their industrial and naval past, the English story is fading. The Royal Navy once called Chatham home. But if the shipwrights who built it returned today, would they even recognise it?

In Walsall, Wolverhampton, and other parts of the West Midlands, tight-knit civic life is being transformed in a single generation. The pubs are gone. In their place: prayer halls, Turkish barbers, and cash-and-carry shops, many little more than money-laundering fronts. The culture that built these towns is vanishing.

Bradford was once known for mills and brass bands. Today, it's known for grooming gangs and blasphemy riots. In parts of town, you can walk for miles without hearing English or seeing a woman without a hijab. The descendants of those who built it are leaving, not by force, but by estrangement.

Luton. Leicester. Tower Hamlets. Ask yourself honestly: Is this still England? Would your grandfather recognise it? Would your great-grandmother feel safe walking through it? Even asking the question now risks professional ruin.

Even the seaside towns are hollowed out. Clacton, Margate, Skegness — once full of working-class families and chip shops, now feel like liminal zones. The hotels house asylum seekers. The high streets are filled with vape shops, foreign signage, and empty storefronts. The people who once filled these places with stories and jokes are gone, or going.

These places weren't just coordinates on a map. They were stories. Anchors. Foundations. Now, too many have become ghost towns, swallowed by cultures that neither know nor care what came before.

This transformation doesn't happen in a vacuum. It coincides with the collapse of religion, family, neighbourhood, and nation. People are told to find identity in brands, ideologies, or the vague abstraction of "global citizenship." But these are not roots. They are placeholders. They accelerate a kind of fluidity where nothing is fixed, sacred, or safe. People become interchangeable. Places lose their character. The individual floats, networked but not connected, stimulated but not grounded.

A teacher in Tower Hamlets said, "I don't even know what culture I'm supposed to teach anymore. Shakespeare is seen as offensive. Half my class doesn't speak English at home." Without shared myth, we don't just lose literature. We lose our moral compass.

Eventually, the soul resists. Some retreat into nostalgia. Others numb themselves. Still others turn to radical ideologies that promise belonging through force. All are responses to the same wound: a spiritual vacuum.

Even politicians feel it. In France, Robert Ménard, mayor of Béziers, said quietly, "France is disappearing." His wife dresses differently. His children don't walk alone at night. His sadness says more than any policy paper.

In Sweden, a statue of a 17th-century king was removed. Officially, it was for "safety." Later, it emerged that the reason was colonial objections, despite the king never having colonised anything. History is now edited for comfort, not truth.

And not all migrants celebrate the change. A Somali mother in Minnesota said, "They're not Somali anymore. But they're not white either. They're lost." Even a Polish plumber who moved to the UK eventually returned home, saying: "I miss Britain more than I miss Poland. Because Britain no longer feels like Britain."

The psychological cost of mass migration is hard to quantify. But you can see it everywhere: rising antidepressant use, declining trust, collapsing civic participation, loneliness, anxiety, cultural fatigue. A silent scream beneath the noise of "progress."

This isn't just about social friction. It's about psychic rupture. We are not blank slates. We are shaped by place, language, ritual, memory, and myth. Remove those, or teach people to pretend they no longer matter, and you don't get harmony. You get disorientation.

Rootlessness doesn't liberate. It disorients. It atomises. If we care about human flourishing, we need to stop treating identity like a trinket. It is the foundation of sanity, of meaning, continuity, and belonging.

Because without belonging, there is no freedom. Only drift. Only isolation mistaken for liberty. Only people wandering through a world of strangers, desperate to remember what home felt like.

Mass migration hollows out the cultural foundations that make a nation feel like home. Cohesion becomes fragmentation. Shared myth becomes mutual suspicion. Neighbours become strangers. Belonging becomes bureaucracy.

It hasn't brought strength. It's brought a fracture. It hasn't brought harmony. It's brought alienation. And even if there were an economic benefit, what's the point if we lose who we are? A country is not a company. A people are not inputs. A nation is not a spreadsheet.

They're told to trade identity for economic growth. That voting for things like Brexit was irrational, emotional, or even ignorant. That they acted against their own interests. But that framing misses the point. They weren't voting against prosperity. They were voting for belonging. For rootedness. For the right to recognise their own country, and still call it home.

They'd rather risk short-term economic pain than permanent cultural dislocation. Because deep down, they know: culture matters more than commerce. Identity isn't a luxury. It's the soil everything else grows from.

We cannot go on like this. The mental, social, and civilisational costs are too high. You can feel it, even if you can't explain it. The dull ache. The rising dread. The sense that something precious has been broken, and no one's coming to fix it.

The institutions don't care. The media gaslights. But there is good news: if we can still remember, we can still return. There are solutions. There is a way back.

13

Reclaiming Control – A Sensible Future for Immigration

C ritics love to pretend that anyone opposed to mass migration wants to build a wall around the country and ban all newcomers forever. That's a lie. The real question has never been whether to have immigration or not. It's how much, from where, and on whose terms.

Immigration done properly can work. Not just economically, but socially, culturally, and morally. For that to happen, it has to be tightly controlled, civilisationally aligned, and unapologetically nation-first.

Look at Denmark. A left-wing government, not a right-wing one, made a sharp U-turn on migration. Why? Because it saw the cost: parallel societies, rising crime, economic dependency, and growing discontent. Denmark introduced some of Europe's strictest immigration policies, including:

- Capping non-Western immigration.
- Tightening asylum eligibility.
- Cutting benefits for those who refuse to integrate.

- Repatriating migrants whose claims are rejected.

The result? Public trust is up. Social cohesion is improving. And unlike the UK, Denmark hasn't had to house 50,000 illegal migrants in hotels [131].

Or take Hungary. Mocked by the EU, scolded by the global press, but safe, stable, and unashamed of itself. Viktor Orbán built a border wall and refused to take part in Brussels' migrant quota schemes. His message was clear: Hungary belongs to Hungarians. Not in a supremacist way, but in the way every country should belong to its people. The result? One of the lowest rates of terror, grooming gangs, or urban violence in Europe [132].

Japan is even more explicit. Fewer than one percent of asylum claims are accepted. Citizenship is almost never granted to foreigners. Mass migration isn't even discussed. Why? Because Japan values what it is and doesn't apologise for wanting to stay that way. And yet Japan isn't poor. It isn't backwards. It isn't a fortress of paranoia. It's modern, advanced, and culturally confident. Diversity didn't build Japan, and they don't pretend otherwise [133].

Poland, far from being some reactionary backwater, has managed migration sanely. They welcomed millions of culturally compatible Ukrainians fleeing war, but rejected EU quotas for Middle Eastern and African migrants. No riots. No grooming gangs. No "diversity is our strength" PR campaigns. Just national self-respect. And it's working. Poland's economy is on a tear, one of the fastest growing in Europe [134].

Switzerland doesn't outsource immigration decisions to international NGOs or EU bureaucrats. Citizenship takes years. You need language, cultural knowledge, a clean record, and the approval of your local community. They've even run national referendums on immigration levels. That's what it looks like when sovereignty means something [135].

Greece, once overwhelmed by waves of migrants, is now taking a hard line. A new draft law threatens prison for anyone who refuses to leave after being denied asylum. Migration Minister Thanos Plevris made the country's position clear: "Don't come here. We will put you in jail or send you back home." In a recent interview, he rejected the idea that most arrivals are vulnerable refugees, stating, "They are mainly men aged between 18 and 30 who are economic migrants... we are not a hotel anymore." Under the proposal, overstaying becomes a criminal offense punishable by at least three years in prison. It is part of a broader push to regain control of Greece's borders [136].

"Show me the incentive and I'll show you the outcome," Charlie Munger once said — a principle that applies as much to immigration as it does to business. When illegal migrants know they can enter a country and receive housing, benefits, and comfort, many will take the risk. That's why the UK is being flooded. But when the incentive changes, when the outcome is prison or deportation, as in Greece's new policy or past U.S. deterrence efforts, the flow slows. Migration is often framed as a moral issue, but at its core, it is driven by predictable human responses to systems of reward and consequence.

Singapore runs a tight ship. Often trotted out as the shining example of a multicultural success story, Singapore is diverse, but not in the way Westerners mean it. Its model is a carefully managed, state-enforced multiculturalism designed to preserve harmony, not celebrate difference for its own sake. Lee Kuan Yew didn't leave identity to chance. He imposed English as the lingua franca, enforced mother tongue education to keep ethnic roots intact, and stamped out competing Chinese dialects in favour of Mandarin to create internal cohesion among the majority.

Housing is engineered by race. Every public housing block must reflect the national ethnic makeup. No ghettos. No enclaves. No racial monocultures. What Western elites would call draconian, Singapore calls common sense.

And immigration? Ruthlessly selective. High skill favoured. Low skill capped. Overstayers jailed. Cultural agitation punished. No mass importing of alien norms or unmanageable demographics. As a result, Singaporeans largely support immigration. Not because they've swallowed diversity dogma, but because the state has proven it can manage it without threatening national cohesion [137].

Singapore isn't proof that mass multiculturalism works. It's proof that tight controls, cultural boundaries, and national identity make limited diversity tolerable. That's the lesson. And the West still refuses to learn it.

South Korea doesn't pretend to be a melting pot. It barely admits migrants. Instead of importing millions, it invests in AI, robotics, and birthrate incentives. It is one of the most ethnically and culturally homogeneous nations on Earth and fiercely proud of it [138].

None of this is complicated. If you want immigration to work, it has to serve the people already there. That means:

- **Low numbers:** No more than society can absorb.
- **High standards:** Cultural compatibility, language, education, and values.
- **Zero tolerance for illegal entry:** One strike and you're out.
- **End the asylum racket:** Scrap the loopholes, fake claims, and economic migrants posing as refugees.
- **No chain migration:** No anchor relatives, no backdoor entries.
- **No dual loyalties:** Citizenship must be earned, not handed out.

- **For Europeans:** Leave the ECHR. Reform the Human Rights Act.
- **Detain and deport illegals:** Process offshore.

Call it controlled migration, assimilation-based immigration, or a nation-first policy. What matters is this: it puts the native population first. As it should. You wouldn't let a stranger rearrange your furniture and call it hospitality. A nation is no less deserving of boundaries than a home.

The principle of national preference holds that a country should prioritise its own citizens, economically, socially, and politically, over non-citizens, including immigrants and foreigners. It rests on a basic civic truth: the first duty of government is to protect and advance the interests of its own people. In practice, this means:

- **Jobs:** Citizens are given priority in hiring, especially in public sector roles or when unemployment is high.
- **Welfare and benefits:** Access to social housing, financial support, and public services is reserved primarily for citizens or for those who have meaningfully contributed to the system.
- **Education:** Publicly funded education programs and scholarships prioritise native born students.
- **Political participation:** Only citizens can vote or hold office, preserving sovereignty and self-determination.

National preference is not hostility toward foreigners. It's a moral order. Just as you owe more to your family than to strangers, you owe more to your fellow citizens than to the rest of the world. To reject this principle is to deny the very idea of nationhood. Without national preference, borders become meaningless, citizenship becomes a formality, and loyalty becomes optional.

We can't keep pretending there's no alternative to demographic chaos. There is. Other nations are doing it. The only thing stopping the West from fixing this is cowardice. The fear of being called names. But history doesn't care about slurs. It only asks one question: Did you protect what mattered?

Controlled immigration is not a fantasy. It is not far right. It is normal. It is moral. And it is the only path back to sanity. Let the others play roulette with their future. We've seen what it costs.

It is not a mystery. We know what works. Across the world, serious nations are protecting their borders, enforcing their values, and defending their future without apology. The question isn't whether a sane immigration policy is possible. It is whether we are still the kind of people who will choose it.

The first step is saying the quiet part out loud. Say what was once unsayable. Mass migration is a civilisational risk. By every measure, it's objectively bad — economically, socially, culturally, and morally. We must shift the conversation, pulling truth back into the realm of the sayable. Politics is downstream of culture. Changing policy can feel impossible, but politics eventually bends to pressure when culture moves first. And we are already seeing it. The Overton window is shifting. People are saying things today that would have ended careers just five years ago. Keir Starmer's recent "island of strangers" speech is a direct response to mounting public pressure and shifting opinion. The spell is breaking. The silence is cracking. Keep pushing.

This is how it begins. Not with permission, but with courage. Not with consensus, but with clarity. Because this was never just a policy debate. It is a civilisational reckoning. One path leads to coherence and continuity. The other to fracture and fade. The choice is still ours, for now. We must choose. What kind of future do we want? And are we brave enough to defend it?

Epilogue

The last time I was in London was in 2022. I hadn't been back in a few years. The buildings were there. The names were the same. But the feeling was different. The bones of the city still stood, but the spirit had drifted. Red brick terraces. Soot-stained stone. The crooked corners of an older world. But the life inside them had changed.

At a crossing, a moped cut through the light. No helmet. No plate. No one chased him. Just motion. A city in fast forward. The church was now a housing office. On the Tube, graffitied windows blurred the city as it passed. The seats were stained. The ads were in six languages. At each station, young men jumped the ticket barriers without a glance. No staff. No resistance. A constant reminder of the decline and ever encroaching anarcho tyranny.

London hadn't been bombed. It hadn't been invaded. It had been administered into something unrecognisable. Not with violence, but with slogans, paperwork, and planning committees. They called it progress. But it felt like forgetting. And I kept walking. Past what was. Through what is. Wondering, not if it can be saved, but if anyone left still wants to.

Western countries are changing rapidly, and not for the better. Mass migration has been imposed without public consent, and the consequences are now impossible to ignore. This isn't natural evolution. It's a transformation born of both design and dysfunction, part engineered, part incompetence, and it's unravelling social cohesion at every level.

Millions have been allowed in who are culturally incompatible with the host nations. Many show no interest in adapting, nor do they make an effort to assimilate. They remain foreign and are encouraged by policy and by ideology to stay that way. Multiculturalism, once sold as enrichment, has become a euphemism for fragmentation.

This is not unique to one country. It is the shared reality across the West. From Britain to France to Germany and beyond, the same pattern repeats: parallel societies, divided loyalties, and entire communities openly hostile to the culture they have chosen to live among.

Public safety has deteriorated. Thousands of women and children have suffered because authorities were too afraid to confront uncomfortable truths. The refusal to name patterns, the institutional cowardice, the moral paralysis - it has cost lives. And it continues.

This is not a civilisation fit for the next generation unless something changes. No amount of slogans or shaming can suppress the truth forever. People see what is happening. They are beginning to speak.

The political class may still be in denial. But the ground is shifting beneath them. The pressure is building. And for many, the only logical path forward is one of hard borders, mass deportations, and the restoration of cultural confidence.

Ultimately, I don't oppose mass migration because I hate others. I oppose it because I love the culture. I want my children to grow up with roots, not rubble. I want our cathedrals to stand, our literature to be read, our streets to feel like home. If that makes me radical, so be it.

Every civilisation faces a choice. To remember who it is, or to forget. To stand, or to dissolve. We are at that moment now. Western civilisation is fast approaching the event horizon. If we don't change course, we're not coming back.

Mass migration has not been an act of compassion. It has been an experiment in erasure. And the people paying the price are not the elites who imposed it, but the ordinary citizens who walk the streets, send their kids to school, wait in hospital queues, and feel their own neighbourhoods slipping away.

You were never asked. You were never told the full cost. And when you noticed, you were told to shut up. Branded a reactionary. But you've seen what mass migration does. It drains the economy. It fractures the culture. It overwhelms infrastructure. It seeds crime, division, and distrust. It atomises the individual, erodes community, and destabilises the psyche. An unravelling of Western identity by people who view rootedness as dangerous and history as guilt. They didn't just open the borders. They opened the soul, and let the West bleed out.

But it's not too late. It is possible to turn back from the abyss. Denmark's government has done an about-face, because it recognises that mass migration is bad for Danes. Sweden, once the poster child for open borders, is now paying migrants to leave. Poland? Virtually zero terror attacks. Why? Because they didn't open their borders to the world. Same with Hungary. They were mocked for building a border fence; now they have safety, cohesion, and cultural confidence. Trump, for all his bombast, radically decreased illegal border crossings in his first three months in office. The lesson is simple. These policies work. What's missing isn't evidence. It's will. The will to protect. The will to say no. The will to put your own people first.

We must say clearly: this is how things are done here. If migrants came for a better life, then they must come to terms with what makes this country better, and it isn't tribalism, theocracy, or imported feuds. It's a hard-won civic culture rooted in law, reason, and individual freedom.

If someone prefers the social norms of the countries they left behind, whether that means medieval gender roles, religious fundamentalism, or institutionalised corruption, then it raises an obvious question: why are they here?

To preserve social cohesion, we must actively dismantle the foundations of parallel societies. That means restricting or banning institutions that entrench cultural separatism: publicly funded Islamic faith schools, face coverings that obscure identity in public life, and foreign-funded religious infrastructure that operates as a state within a state. We will not allow Sharia courts, sectarian politics, or cousin marriage. We will no longer fund interpreters in public institutions. English will be the language of civic life. Integration isn't optional. Like Denmark, we should adopt a policy of deliberate, enforced assimilation.

We must also stop indulging performative grievances. If you're offended by the norms of the society you chose to live in, you are free to leave. The West cannot become a dumping ground for those who reject its values while exploiting its benefits.

We must recover moral confidence. There are places in the world, riddled with corruption, violence, and regression, that reflect the very values some migrants insist on importing. If that's the society they want, it already exists. They are welcome to return to it. What they should not be allowed to do is recreate it in the West.

This isn't about race or religion. It's about civilisation versus anti-civilisation. It's about the right of a nation to defend its cultural software from being overwritten. If that means removals on a mass scale, then so be it. Multiculturalism was a utopian idea. Reality demands borders, not just physical, but moral and cultural ones too.

End illegal immigration. Deport those who came unlawfully. Strip out every incentive to come. No benefits. No hotels. No fast tracks to citizenship. Tighten legal migration to a trickle, based on compatibility and contribution. Scrap the broken asylum system. Make refugees find help closer to their home or compatible nations. And above all, reclaim our story. Not as an apology, but as a birthright. Because policy alone isn't enough. You need belief. Pride. Purpose. Because no law will hold if the people enforcing it have already surrendered in spirit. This isn't just about immigration. It's about meaning.

Can a nation survive if it no longer believes it has the right to exist? Can a culture endure if it teaches its children to be ashamed of it? Can a people remain free if they are told their very identity is hate? We must reassert the right to exist, not as economic units, but as a people. Not as a market, but as a culture. Not as a flag of convenience, but as an inheritance of memory and belonging.

We ask why the West no longer builds anything beautiful. Why our cities feel increasingly soulless and in a state of managed decline. Why everything is flat, grey, and utilitarian. When asked why great Gothic cathedrals are no longer built, nineteenth-century poet Heinrich Heine explained: "The men of old times had convictions; we modern men have only opinions, and more than these are needed to raise cathedrals." We abandoned belief. Our mythos. Our sense of who we are and what we're here to do. And with it, we lost the will to build anything that lasts. Anything grand. Anything sacred.

People who are unsure of their identity will never build monuments to it. They'll build shopping malls. Data centres. Bureaucracies. They'll forget how to aim upward, because they no longer remember what they're reaching for. If we want to build cathedrals again, literal or symbolic, we need to become a people capable of building them. That means clarity. Conviction. And boundaries. Because identity doesn't survive by accident. It survives by design.

Our civilisation cannot survive if it keeps appeasing those who despise it. You cannot coexist with ideologies that view tolerance as weakness. Appeasement doesn't buy peace. It only delays collapse. If we don't defend the values that built the West, we will lose them. Not all at once, but one compromise at a time. We must become unapologetic stewards of the West.

But after we say "enough," what then? What does a restored West actually look like? It looks like a West that remembers what it is, not just what it isn't. A West that doesn't flinch at its own reflection. That doesn't apologise for its beauty, its brilliance, its order, or its myths. A West that teaches its children pride without arrogance, memory without shame, and duty without coercion.

It means borders, not just as lines on a map, but as cultural boundaries. It means assimilation with expectations. If you come, you come to join, not to reshape. Not to import your homeland, but to embrace ours.

It means ending the cult of sameness. That spirit leaching belief that all cultures are equal, all values interchangeable, all people just economic widgets waiting to be shuffled around by global planners. They aren't. We aren't.

It means reviving the old virtues: courage, loyalty, restraint, reverence. It means truth spoken without fear. Art that elevates. Religion that grounds. Education that transmits, not deconstructs. It means mythos. A remembered West. A culture that sings again, of Chartres and Canterbury, of the Odyssey and the Psalms, of Magna Carta and Gettysburg and the cathedrals of light we once built both in stone and in spirit.

It doesn't mean nostalgia. It means rooted modernity. Strong families and strong stories. Border walls. Bach. iPhones. Inheritance. The restored West is not a museum. It's a civilisation with a memory. One that builds again. Believes again. Binds again. And it starts by saying: we are not ashamed.

Because this is not just a fight against something. It's a fight for something. For order. For home. For meaning. For villages where children can play until dusk. For classrooms where Shakespeare isn't a hate crime. For streets where women can walk without fear. For churches that ring out, not hide in silence. For the right to feel like a citizen, not a trespasser, in the country your grandparents built.

Ultimately, my opposition to mass migration doesn't come from hatred of the outsider, but from love of the West and the culture that I love. It's not driven by resentment. It's driven by reverence. Like Roger Scruton, I believe politics, at its best, is a mechanism for conserving the things we love: the architecture, the literature, the rituals, the landscapes, the memories. The quiet beauty of ordinary things.

Roger Scruton once wrote, "Conservatism is the philosophy of attachment. We are attached to the things we love, and wish to protect them against decay."

That's it. That's the heart of it. I don't want to shut people out. I want to hold something sacred in. Because I've seen it, I've felt it, and I believe, deeply, that it's worth preserving.

I want honesty boxes by the roadside, wooden crates stacked with eggs or apples, a tin for coins, and the quiet trust that no one will take without paying. I want parks where parents don't have to constantly scan for threats, where kids can run barefoot through the grass and leave their scooters by the bench without them vanishing in five minutes. I want to walk into a corner shop and be greeted in English, not with suspicion, not behind a scratched plexiglass screen, but with a nod and a shared cultural rhythm. I want high streets with real butchers, bakeries, family-run florists, not shell businesses and vape shops run by men who look at you like you don't belong. I want streets calm enough for conversation, not swallowed by packs of migrant Deliveroo drivers racing through red lights on mopeds with no plates, weaving between strollers like it's a chase scene. Shops that don't need CCTV covering every angle, or have to chain the patio chairs to the table legs at night, like it's a prison yard. Just normal shops. Normal people. A place held together by trust, not tension.

When I see a Spitfire, a thing of beauty in its own right, I don't just admire it. I feel something. A kind of reverence. It's not just a machine. It's an artefact of courage, sacrifice, and ingenuity, an embodiment of what my people once achieved and fought to preserve. Others feel the same way about Lincoln Cathedral. Or a steam locomotive. Or even the silent stones of Stonehenge. These aren't just structures. They're spiritual landmarks. Proof that this land is not just dirt, but history. Not just territory, but home.

That bond, between people, ancestors, and place, is not trivial. It's what makes a homeland more than a neoliberal grazing strip. It's what makes people care. Because they're not just invested economically, they're invested spiritually and biologically in what happens to the land their ancestors bled for.

What makes a place feel like home isn't just buildings or passports. It's belonging. Familiarity. That subtle web of shared reference, rhythm, and ritual, the shorthand of a people who know each other without speaking. It's the old songs on the radio that your dad hummed in the kitchen. The accent of your childhood teachers. The street names that carry stories. The jokes you don't have to explain. It's knowing what someone means when they say "Blue Peter," or hum the EastEnders theme tune. It's shouting at the telly during a World Cup match and knowing the whole street is doing the same.

England is not a contract. It is a covenant. A shared memory etched into the hills and hedgerows, into village rituals and the books on your grandfather's shelf. You don't join it by paperwork. You join it by understanding it in your bones. It's the cadence of the evening news. The roast on Sunday. The quiet reverence of Remembrance Day. The strange national rituals that don't make sense unless you grew up inside them, and make perfect sense if you did. Identity is not an abstraction. It's not some bureaucratic checkbox. It's music, memory, myth. It's the familiar smell of your nan's cooking. The sound of a local choir singing hymns that no one wrote down, but everyone seems to know. It's walking into a pub and feeling, instantly, that you belong, not because you're known, but because you're known to be from here.

Strip that away, and what's left? A postcode. A tax bracket. An airport with people moving through it. No community. No continuity. No sense that the people around you see the world in the same basic way. Identity is what allows trust. It's what allows silence to feel companionable. It's what makes a crowd feel like a congregation. And it's beautiful, not because it excludes, but because it binds. That's why this matters. Why people mourn the loss of their country before it disappears. Because they feel the chords snapping. The shared songs fading. The spell breaking. We are not machines. We are not interchangeable. And a home is not just where you sleep, it's where you know who you are.

And we should be proud of the West. Fiercely proud. This is the civilisation that gave the world Socrates and Shakespeare. That birthed the cathedral and the symphony. That carved order out of chaos, raised science from superstition, and wrestled with the great questions of existence, not with bombs or dogma, but with reason, art, and truth.

The West is not perfect. But it is exceptional. It's the home of the Magna Carta and the moon landing. Of Newton's laws and Beethoven's 9th. Of the Sistine Chapel and the printing press. The West didn't just build empires. It built ideas that outlived them: liberty, dignity, conscience, inquiry.

It gave us the concept of the individual. The rule of law. The belief that truth exists and can be known. That beauty matters. That life should be more than survival. These aren't abstractions. They're the foundation of every right we take for granted. Every book we read. Every bridge we cross. Every piece of music that stirs the soul.

To lose the West isn't just to lose a place. It's to lose the inheritance of generations. To forget who we are and what we're capable of. We are the heirs of a thousand-year fire. It is ours to tend, or to let go out. The flame hasn't gone out yet. But it flickers. And what we do now will decide whether it's rekindled or lost forever.

The West is worth defending not because it's flawless, but because it's ours. Because it is the only civilisation in history that built both Athens and Florence, the telescope and the symphony, the republic and the Renaissance. Because without the West, the world goes dark.

The future is not yet written. The line between decline and renewal is thin, but it still exists. And the choice is still ours to make. It's not too late. But it will be soon.

So remember who you are. Reclaim what you've inherited. Honor the past, and light the way forward.

References

Chapter 1

1. YouGov. *British Attitudes Toward Immigration*. Survey conducted in 2025.

2. IFOP. *French Public Opinion on Immigration*. National survey, December 2023.

3. Infratest dimap for ARD. *German Attitudes on Deportation Policy*. Poll conducted January 2024.

4. Gallup. *Trends in U.S. Attitudes Toward Immigration and Border Control*. Ongoing annual polling, 2000–2025.

5. Environics Institute. *Focus Canada Survey: Immigration and Refugee Policy*. Fall 2024.

6. Pollara Strategic Insights. *Canadian Views on Immigration and Culture, 2002–2025*. Summary data compiled from annual polling.

Chapter 2

7. Office for National Statistics, "Long—term international migration, provisional: year ending December 2023," *UK Government*, May 2024.

8. *Reuters*, "Annual migration to UK fell last year but remains high," May 23, 2024.

9. Migration Observatory, "Non—EU nationals made up 85% of immigration in 2023," *University of Oxford*, 2024.

10. Office for National Statistics, "Why do people come to the UK?," *UK Government*, 2023.

11. Migration Observatory, "The Impact of Migration on UK Population Growth," *University of Oxford*, 2023.

12. *BBC News*, "Channel migrant crossings rise by 25% in 2024," June 2025.

13. Office for National Statistics, "Ethnic group and religion by age and sex, London," *2021 Census, UK Government*, 2022.

14. Matthew Goodwin, "How Immigration Will Change Britain Forever," *UnHerd*, November 2022.

15. Federal Office for Migration and Refugees, "Migration Report 2023," *Government of Germany*, 2024.

16. Central Statistics Office, "Population and Migration Estimates, April 2023," *Government of Ireland*, August 2023.

17. Immigration, Refugees and Citizenship Canada, "Canada – Permanent Resident Admissions 2023," *Government of Canada*, 2024.

18. Statistics Canada, "Canada's population estimates: Third quarter 2024," *Government of Canada*, 2024.

19. Statistics Sweden, "Population by country of birth and background, 2023," *Government of Sweden*, 2024.

20. U.S. Customs and Border Protection, "Southwest Land Border Encounters FY2023," *Department of Homeland Security*, 2024.

21. United States Census Bureau, "Race and Hispanic Origin in the 10 Largest U.S. Cities: 2020," *U.S. Census Bureau*, 2021.

22. Office for National Statistics. *Ethnicity and the criminal justice system statistics*, 2020.

23. Greater London Authority. *London Datastore – Ethnic Group Population Projections*, 2021.

24. Metropolitan Police. Statement by Cressida Dick on youth knife crime, reported in multiple outlets including The Times (2021): "Young black men aged 16 to 24 make up 47% of knife crime suspects in London."

Chapter 3

25. *The Guardian*, "The Canada experiment: is this the world's first 'postnational' country?", January 4, 2017.

26. Christopher Caldwell, "A New Chapter in the Haitian Nightmare," *City Journal*, Autumn 2021.

27. Hua Hsu, "The Black and White and Brown Faces of Les Bleus," *The New Yorker*, July 16, 2018.

Chapter 4

28. Stephan Schiffels et al., "The Anglo-Saxon migration and the formation of the early English gene pool," *Nature*, 2022 (finding 73 ± 4 % Y-chromosomes distinct from Bronze/Iron Age England).

29. Theodore Roosevelt, speech to American Defense Society, January 3, 1919: "We have room for but one flag... one language... one sole loyalty to the American people."

Chapter 5

30. Nippon.com and FPRI analysis, "Japan accepted refugee status for 190 people in 2024 (≈1.5 percent approval rate)," April 2025.

31. European media coverage, Poland and Hungary criticized for immigration policy similar to Japan's, 2024–2025.

32. Office for National Statistics, "Religion, England and Wales: 2021," 2022.

33. Office for National Statistics, "Deaths related to terrorism in the UK, 1992–2022," February 2022.

34. MI5/MI5 CONTEST report, "80 percent of live terrorism investigations in 2023 were Islamist," 2023.

35. UK Ministry of Justice, "Prison population by religion, March 2024," 2024.

36. UK crime data analysis, "Child sexual exploitation and grooming: ethnic breakdown," 2022–2024.

37. Pew Research Center, "British Muslim attitudes on Hamas, October 2023 survey," December 2023.

38. UK Home Office, "Female genital mutilation in England and Wales: annual statistics," 2024.

39. UK National Health Service, "Birth defect rates by maternal ethnicity," 2023.

40. French legislation, "Ban on full—face coverings," 2010 legislation in effect 2011.

41. Danish Parliament, "Ban on full—face coverings," 2018.

42. Danish proposal, "Expansion of full—face ban to schools and universities," 2025.

43. Dutch government restrictions, "Full—face coverings limited in hospitals, transport, schools," 2019.

44. Brunel University post—Brexit migration study, "Net migration reached 764,000 in 2022 and record levels post—Brexit," 2024.

Chapter 6

45. UNHCR and multiple reports, "Lebanon hosts over 1.1 million Syrian refugees, straining state capacity," 2024.

46. ICWA, "Palestinian and Syrian refugee influx has intensified sectarian tensions and weakened Lebanon's state cohesion," 2022.

Chapter 7

47. Institute for Economics & Peace. *Global Peace Index 2023: Measuring Peace in a Complex World.*

48. Zhang, B. "Why China Does Not Promote Immigration." *Asia Times*, 2021.

49. Traynor, I. "Molenbeek: the Brussels borough linked to terror." *The Guardian*, 2015.

50. *Libération.* "Je vis en France, mais je ne suis pas Français." 2018

51. Kerbaj, R. "Sharia courts rule on sex and child custody." *The Times (UK)*, 2015

52. Murray, D. *The Strange Death of Europe: Immigration, Identity, Islam.* Bloomsbury Publishing, 2017

53. Putnam, R. D. "E Pluribus Unum: Diversity and Community in the Twenty—first Century." *Scandinavian Political Studies*, vol. 30, no. 2, 2007, pp. 137–174.

54. Goodhart, D. *The British Dream: Successes and Failures of Post—war Immigration.* Atlantic Books, 2013

55. Bittles, A. H. *Consanguinity in Context.* Cambridge University Press, 2013.
— Supports the claim that ~66% of marriages in Pakistan are between blood relatives.

56. MacEoin, D. *Sharia Law or 'One Law for All'?* Civitas: Institute for the Study of Civil Society, 2009. — Reports that among British Pakistanis, approximately 55% of marriages are between first cousins.

57. *Born in Bradford Cohort Study*, University of York. (2013).

58. Bittles, A. H. *Consanguinity in Context.* Cambridge University Press, 2013.

59. Woodley of Menie, M. A., et al. "The dysgenic fertility effect in the UK." *Intelligence*, vol. 69, 2018, pp. 10–17.

60. [54] MacEoin, D. *Sharia Law or 'One Law for All'?* Civitas: Institute for the Study of Civil Society, 2009.

61. Lee Kuan Yew. *The Wit and Wisdom of Lee Kuan Yew.* Editions Didier Millet, 1997.

62. [54] Public Accounts Committee. *Child Sexual Exploitation and the Response to Localised Grooming.* UK Parliament, 2013.

63. Copsey, N. "Ethnic Bloc Voting and Party Strategy in the UK." *British Politics Review*, vol. 15, no. 2, 2020, pp. 20–22.

64. *Dawn News.* "UK MPs Push for Airport in Mirpur." 2023

65. Kingsley, P. "In Brussels, Fear of Being 'Erased.'" *New York Times*, 2016.

66. Tibi, B. *The Challenge of Fundamentalism: Political Islam and the New World Disorder.* University of California Press, 2002.

67. Zakaria, F. *The Future of Freedom: Illiberal Democracy at Home and Abroad.* W. W. Norton & Company, 2001.

68. Hussain, A., & Bagguley, P. "Citizenship, Ethnicity and the Second Generation: British Pakistani Youth." *Sociology*, vol. 39, no. 3, 2005, pp. 407–425.

69. New York State Assembly. "Assemblymember Zohran K. Mamdani – Biography." 2023.

70. Hennepin County Elections. "Precinct—Level Results and Analysis." 2020.

71. Rindermann, H. *Cognitive Capitalism: Human Capital and the Wellbeing of Nations.* Cambridge University Press, 2018.

72. De Standaard. "Islam Party wants Sharia law in Belgium." 2018.

73. The Times. "Lutfur Rahman re—elected in Tower Hamlets despite fraud scandal." 2022.

74. Elections Canada. "Language Profiles in Candidate Materials." 2021.

75. CBC News. "Brampton parade re—enacts Indira Gandhi assassination." 2023.

76. National Post. "Posters Accusing Indian Diplomats of Murder Spark Tensions in Canada." 2023

77. House of Commons of Canada. *Diaspora Politics and Foreign Influence*. 2022.

78. Canadian Security Intelligence Service. *Foreign Interference and Diaspora Politics in Canada*. 2023.

Chapter 8

79. Statistics Canada. "Gross Domestic Product, income and expenditure: Second quarter 2023." *The Daily*, Aug 30, 2023.

80. Vox. Bernie Sanders interview: "Open borders? That's a Koch brothers proposal." July 2015.

81. Collier, Paul. *Exodus: How Migration is Changing Our World*. Oxford University Press, 2013.

82. Borjas, George J. "The Labour Market Impact of Immigration: A Meta—Analysis." NBER Working Paper 27842, 2020.

83. Borjas, George J. "The Labour Demand Curve Is Downward Sloping." *Quarterly Journal of Economics*, 2003.

84. National Academies of Sciences. *The Economic and Fiscal Consequences of Immigration*, 2017.

85. OECD. *Indicators of Immigrant Integration 2023: Settling In*.

86. Dustmann, C. and Frattini, T. "The Fiscal Effects of Immigration to the UK." *The Economic Journal*, 2014.

87. *The Telegraph*. "Benefits Claims by Households with Foreign Nationals," May 30, 2025.

88. Reuters. "Fact Check: UK Spending on Hotels for Asylum Seekers," June 20, 2025.

89. ONS Census 2021; Muslim Council of Britain; IFS *Race and Ethnicity in the UK*, 2022.

90. Institute for Fiscal Studies. *IFS Deaton Review: Race and Ethnicity*, 2022.

91. *The Guardian*. "Afghan data leak timeline," July 16, 2025.

92. *The Local Denmark*. "Non—Western migrants cost Denmark 31bn kroner," Oct 15, 2021.

93. Swedish Ministry of Finance. Annual fiscal report, 2022.

94. Government of Sweden. *Integration Policy Progress Report*, 2020.

95. Dutch Ministry of Social Affairs. "Lifetime Fiscal Impact of Non—Western Migrants," 2018.

96. Heritage Foundation. *The Fiscal Cost of Unlawful Immigrants*, 2013.

97. California Legislative Analyst's Office. "Spending on Services for Unauthorized Immigrants," 2022.

98. INSEE (France). "Labour Market Outcomes by Nationality," 2023.

99. French Ministry of Labour. Quarterly Employment Bulletin, Q1 2024.

100.　　OFII. Annual Report, 2023.

101.　　Bill Curry, *Canada has spent $1.1 billion on hotel rooms for asylum seekers since 2017, Ottawa says*, The Globe and Mail, July 23, 2024.

102.　　Borjas, George J. et al. "The Impact of Immigration on Native Wages," NBER Working Paper.

Chapter 9

103.　　Dimant, Eugen. *On Peer Effects: Behavioral Contagion of (Un)ethical Behavior and the Role of Social Identity*. CESifo Working Paper No. 8263, 2019.

104.　　103. Germany's Federal Police. 2022 crime data, including analysis of group sexual assaults by nationality. Reported in *Bild* and *Die Welt*

105.   BBC News. "Lawangeen Abdulrahimzai jailed for life for murder of Thomas Roberts." January 2023.

106.   Reuters. "Afghan migrant convicted of rape and murder of student Maria Ladenburger in Freiburg." March 2018.

107.   Deutsche Welle. "Germany: Afghan asylum seeker sentenced to life for murder of ex—girlfriend in Kandel." August 2018.

108.   France24. "France teacher attack: Who was Samuel Paty and what happened to him?" October 2020.

109.   Bundeskriminalamt (BKA). *Polizeiliche Kriminalstatistik 2023*. Summary figures reported via *The Critic*, April 2024.

110.   Nordrhein—Westfalen Ministry of the Interior. *2023 Regional Crime Report*.

111.   Cologne Police Department and federal reports on the 2015–2016 New Year's Eve mass assaults in Cologne.

112.   Swedish Ministry of Justice. *Brott och Straff: Rapport 2005*.

113.   Brå (Swedish National Council for Crime Prevention). *Sexualbrott i Sverige 2006–2018*.

114.   SVT Nyheter. "58 procent av dem som dömts för våldtäkt är födda utomlands." July 2018.

115.   Austria Interior Ministry. *2023 Vienna Crime Statistics*.

116.   Oslo Police Department. *Anmeldte voldtekter i Oslo 2010–2011*. Cited in *Aftenposten*.

117.   Finnish Police and Ministry of Justice. Crime statistics, 2021.

118.   Swiss Federal Statistics Office and Canton Zürich crime data, 2017–2020.

119.   UK Ministry of Justice. FOI data released in *The Telegraph*, 2025.

120.   Survation. *Majority of Women Feel Unsafe in London and Want Further Safety Measures Implemented*. April 2025. Commissioned by ITV News.

121.   UK Home Office. *Group—Based Child Sexual Exploitation: Characteristics of Offending*. December 2020.

122.   Whistleblower testimony cited in *The Times*, *Mail on Sunday*, and survivor organizations.

123.   7 July 2005 London bombings. Public source summary based on official reports and news archives.

124.   Manchester Arena bombing. Public source summary from 2017 coverage.

125.   French Justice Ministry and penal system data. Estimates reported in *Le Monde* and *Le Figaro*.

126.   U.S. Department of Justice and FBI case files on the 2015 San Bernardino attack.

127.   CBC News. "Teen who fatally stabbed 3 girls at U.K. dance studio sentenced to life in prison." July 3, 2025.

128.   BBC News. "Delivery drivers jailed for sexually assaulting 14 year old girl." June 28, 2025

129.   *Mail+* (Scottish Edition). "Asylum seeker who raped girl, 15, was not aware of cultural differences, claims his lawyer." January 2023.

130.   BBC News. "Mum jailed for tweet about migrants after Southport stabbings." June 13, 2025.

Chapter 13

131.   "Denmark Tightens Immigration Laws to Promote Integration," *Reuters*, April 2022.

132.   "Hungary Builds Border Fence to Curb Migration," *BBC News*, September 2015.

133.   "Japan's Strict Refugee Policy Under Fire," *Nikkei Asia*, February 2023.

134.   "Poland's Migration Policy in the Face of the Ukrainian Refugee Crisis," *Migration Policy Institute*, May 2022.

135.   "How Switzerland Manages Immigration through Direct Democracy," *The Economist*, October 2020.

136.   Reuters. (2025, July 20). *Greece plans to jail migrants who refuse to leave under new draft law, says minister*. Reuters.

137.   "Singapore's Managed Multiculturalism," *Brookings Institution*, August 2020.

138.   "South Korea's Response to Labour Shortages: Invest in AI, Not Immigration," *World Economic Forum*, January 2023.

Printed in Dunstable, United Kingdom